STUDY GUIDE

Dust to Glory

An Overview of the Bible with R.C. Sproul

New Testament

LIGONIER MINISTRIES

Renew your Mind.

LIGONIER.ORG | 800.435.4343

Old Testament Editors: Chris Donato, Robert Rothwell, Keith Mathison, and Peter Nadeau
Copyright © 2004, 2010 Ligonier Ministries
P.O. Box 547500, Orlando, Florida 32854
E-mail: info@ligonier.org
All rights reserved.
No reproduction of this work without permission.
Printed in the United States of America
Scripture is taken from the *Holy Bible: The New King James Version*. Copyright 1979, 1980, 1982
By Thomas Nelson, Inc. Used by permission.
All rights reserved.

Contents

Introduction

Our Lord declared that "man shall not live by bread alone, but by every Word that proceeds from the mouth of God" (Matt. 4:4). The Bible is that Word by which we are to live.

I believe that *Dust to Glory* is the most important teaching tool Ligonier has produced. It is our prayer that it will serve you in your desire to grow in the knowledge and love of God. As Christians, we are called to be people of the Word. My hope is that *Dust to Glory* will encourage, stimulate, and assist you in your goal to dissect the Scriptures so that the Scriptures may, in turn, dissect you (Heb. 4:12).

Sincerely,
R.C. Sproul

31

The Intertestamental Period

MESSAGE INTRODUCTION

The Gospels open the New Testament with the announcement that the fullness of time had come and God was about to reveal His Messiah to the world. The coming of the promised Redeemer ended a four hundred year period of silence between the Old and New Testaments. God brought His people from an old to a new covenant and the words of the prophets began to see their fulfillment in Jesus the Messiah. In this lecture, Dr. Sproul discusses the Intertestamental Period.

SCRIPTURE READING

Zephaniah, Haggai, Zechariah, Malachi

LEARNING OBJECTIVES

1. To describe the historical period between the Old and New Testaments.

2. To outline the major empires that controlled Palestine during the Intertestamental Period.

3. To track the evolution of Judaism during the Intertestamental Period.

QUOTATIONS

The four hundred years between the prophet Malachi and the birth of Christ were important years in the history of Israel. During this time, the nation winessed the fall of the Perisan Empire, the rise and fall of the Greek Empire, and the rise of the Roman Empire. But Israel did not witness these events from afar. The crises and suffering experienced during these years led to the production of numerous writings. In these writings, the

hopes of the Jewish people are expressed. They look forward to the coming of a Messiah, one who would judge their enemies and establish the kingdom of God forever.
                                                                —Keith Mathison

LECTURE OUTLINE

A. The Gospels open the New Testament with the announcement of the pleroma, which is the "fullness of time".

   1. The history of redemption reaches a period of fruition with the advent of Christ in the New Testament.

   2. The Old Testament recounts the long period of time in which God was preparing the world for the coming of His Son.

B. The historical record of the Old Testament closes approximately four hundred years before the opening events of the New Testament.

C. The reconstruction of the walls of Jerusalem was completed in 445 BC under the leadership of Nehemiah.

   1. The small post-exilic Jewish nation struggled to survive in the ancient Near East.

   2. Palestine continued to be a hotly contested geo-political land-bridge between the major military powers.

D. The Persian Empire remained the dominant power in the Ancient Near East until 331 BC when it was conquered by Alexander the Great.

E. Alexander the Great had completed his conquest of the Persians at the age of 24.

   1. Alexander was the son of Philip of Macedon and the pupil of the Greek philosopher Aristotle.

   2. Aristotle was the pupil of Plato and Plato was the pupil of Socrates.

F. Aristotle emphasized unity and a search for the system that would unify all branches of knowledge.

   • A large host of scientists and philosophers accompanied Alexander in his conquest of the ancient world to help Aristotle advance his studies.

G. Throughout his empire, Alexander emphasized Hellenism, which was the spread of Greek language and culture.

   1. Alexander's empire would be unified in language, customs, and philosophy.

2. The New Testament was written in Greek due in large part to the successful Hellenization of the ancient world.

H. Alexander died in 327 BC in Babylon and his kingdom was divided among four generals.

I. Eventually the Grecian empire was divided between the two dynasties of the Ptolemies and the Seleucids.
1. The Ptolemies ruled Palestine and Egypt and the Seleucids ruled Syria and Asia Minor.

2. Ptolemy I annexed Palestine in 320 BC.

3. Palestine was taken by Antiochus III (223–187 BC) for the Seleucids in 198 BC.

4. Antiochus accelerated the process of Hellenization in Palestine.

J. The process of Hellenization was fiercely opposed by conservative Jews.
1. The Hassidim or "the pious ones" fought in vain against the growing Greek influence on the Jews.

2. Many groups struggled to maintain the purity of their traditions including the Pharisees who appear frequently in the New Testament.

3. The Pharisees or "separated ones" were to be zealous for the covenant and obedient to every aspect of the law.

4. The Pharisees degenerated into self-righteous legalism and ritualism by the time of Christ.

K. Antiochus IV Epiphanes (175–164 BC) became king of the Seleucids in 175 BC.
1. Epiphany means "manifestation" and Antiochus IV Epiphanes was considered to be the "manifest god".

2. Antiochus was driven to insanity in his latter years.

L. Antiochus IV Epiphanes fulfilled the Old Testament prophecy of the "abomination that makes desolate" (Dan. 9:27).
1. Antiochus IV Epiphanes inaugurated a radically anti-Jewish program in Palestine and was nicknamed Antiochus Epimanes which means "insane" or "madman".

2. Antiochus made observance of the Sabbath, circumcision, and possessing a copy of the Hebrew Scriptures each a capital offense.

3. Antiochus had a pig sacrificed on the sacred altar in the Jerusalem temple in 167 BC.

M. The Maccabean revolt began in 164 BC.
   1. A devout Jew named Mattathias who had five sons rose up in protest against the abominations of Antiochus.

   2. The Maccabean family launched a guerrilla war against the forces of Antiochus.

   3. After the death of Mattathias, leadership of the revolt fell to his third son Judas "the Hammer" Maccabeus.

   4. The Maccabean revolt succeeded in securing concessions from Antiochus including religious freedom and opening the temple for religious ceremonies.

   5. The reopening and rededication of the temple is still commemorated today in the Jewish holiday of Hanukkah.

N. The Jews secured their freedom in 142 BC from foreign powers and remained independent until 63 BC.
   1. The Romans conquered Palestine in 63 BC under the command of Pompeii.

   2. Pompeii was a member of Rome's first great triumvirate.

O. An Idumean chieftain named Herod the Great was appointed as a local king over the Jews in 40 BC.
   1. Herod the Great founded a dynasty and rebuilt the Jerusalem temple.

   2. Herod was appointed by Marc Anthony and Octavius or Caesar Augustus.

P. The New Testament opens with the Jewish people languishing under the domination of the Romans and an oppressive king.

BIBLE STUDY

Although no inspired books of Scripture were written during the Intertestamental period, many other non-canonical books were written. Some of these are contained within the Apocrypha. These books are not inspired Scripture, but like other merely human writings, they can be helpful for understanding the historical and religious developments that occurred during these four hundred years between the end of the Old Testament and the beginning of the New. Among the most helpful of these books for understanding the historical developments are 1 and 2 Maccabees. Those interested in the religious and literary developments of this era may also want to read some of the other apocryphal books such as Tobit, Judith, or the Wisdom of Solomon.

DISCUSSION

1. Is it important for Christians to have some understanding of the events that transpired in the four hundred years before Jesus was born? Is it necessary? Why might it be helpful to the interpretation of the New Testament?

2. The apocryphal books were formally declared to be part of the canon by the Roman Catholic Church at the Council of Trent in 1546. The Westminster Confession of Faith, on the contrary, states that these books "are no part of the canon of the scripture" and that they are to be used no differently "than other human writings" (I:3). The Belgic Confession says regarding the Apocrypha: "All which the church may read and take instruction from, so far as they agree with the canonical books . . ." (Art. VI). Is it appropriate to publish these apocryphal books with the biblical books as was done, for example, in the Geneva Bible and the 1611 King James Bible, even if they are published in a separate section apart from the Old and New Testament books? Why or why not?

3. The Reformers rejected granting the apocryphal books a canonical authority they did not and do not have, but they did not disapprove of the reading of these books. Many Protestants, however, seem to have gone beyond rightly rejecting their canonical status and have ignored these books completely. How may Christians use books, such as those in the Apocrypha, rightly today?

FOR FURTHER STUDY

de Silva, David A. *Introducing the Apocrypha: Message, Context, and Significance*
Hayes, John H. and Sara Mandell. *The Jewish People in Classical Antiquity*
Helger, Larry R. *Exploring Jewish Literature of the Second Temple Period*

32

John the Baptist

MESSAGE INTRODUCTION

John the Baptist is one of the most significant figures in the New Testament. He was given the charge of preparing the people for the coming Messiah and announcing the imminence of the kingdom of God. Through a ministry of preaching and baptism in the wilderness, John prepared hearts for the ministry of Jesus and condemned the religious authorities for their hypocrisy and hard hearts. Turning the hearts of the fathers to the children and the children to their fathers, John the Baptist revived the prophetic ministry of Elijah and fulfilled Malachi's prophecy of a coming prophet. In this lecture, Dr. Sproul discusses the character and career of John the Baptist.

SCRIPTURE READING

Matthew 3, 11, 14:1–12; Mark 1; Luke 1, 3, 7; John 1, 3

LEARNING OBJECTIVES

1. To discuss the role of John the Baptist in the story of redemption.

2. To interpret Malachi's prophecy of the return of Elijah the prophet.

3. To describe the message and means of John the Baptist's ministry.

QUOTATIONS

John's interest is in the Christ and in nothing less. . . . He brings out the greatness of the one who was to come by referring to his own personal unworthiness. He was not worthy to loose the thongs of the great one's sandal. Loosing the sandal was the task of a slave;

a disciple could not be expected to perform it. There is a rabbinic saying: "Every service which a slave performs for his master shall a disciple do for his teacher except the loosing of his sandal-thong." John selects the very task that the rabbinic saying stresses as too menial for any disciple, and declares himself unworthy to perform it. He is unworthy of the most menial of tasks for the one who was to come after him. Humility could scarcely take a lower place.

—Leon Morris

LECTURE OUTLINE

A. Jesus identifies John the Baptist as the most important prophet under the Old Covenant.
1. "I tell you, among those born of women none is greater than John. Yet the one who is least in the kingdom of God is greater than he" (Luke 7:28).

2. John, as one under the Old Covenant, was part of the period of preparation before the breakthrough of the kingdom of God.

3. Those who live under the New Covenant enjoy a greater state of blessedness than any of those who live under the Old Covenant.

B. One of the most under-appreciated figures in the New Testament is John the Baptist.
1. Only two of the four gospels recount the birth of Jesus, whereas all four discuss the coming of John the Baptist.

2. "The beginning of the gospel of Jesus Christ, the Son of God. As it is written in Isaiah the prophet, 'Behold, I send my messenger before your face, who will prepare your way, the voice of one crying in the wilderness: Prepare the way of the Lord, make his paths straight,' John appeared, baptizing in the wilderness and proclaiming a baptism of repentance for the forgiveness of sins" (Mark 1:1–4).

3. Mark opens his gospel by discussing the significance of John the Baptist.

4. John is mentioned more frequently than Jesus by the ancient pagan historians.

C. The appearance of John was very significant because the voice of prophecy had been silent for four hundred years until his coming.

D. The prophet Malachi spoke of the coming of John in the last prophecy in the Old Testament.

1. "Behold, I will send you Elijah the prophet before the great and awesome day of the Lord comes. And he will turn the hearts of fathers to their children and the hearts of children to their fathers, lest I come and strike the land with a decree of utter destruction" (Malachi 4:5–6).

2. The prophets spoke frequently about a coming day of the Lord in which there would be an outpouring of God's wrath for the wicked and redemption for the faithful.

3. Malachi prophesied that before the Day of the Lord an Elijah would come to the people.

E. After an absence in prophecy for four hundred years, John the Baptist came out of the wilderness dressed and preaching in the manner of the prophet Elijah.
   - John's simple message was to repent for the kingdom of God was at hand.

F. The message of the Old Testament prophets was that the kingdom of God will come some day; whereas John's message was that the kingdom was at hand or very near.
   1. John declared that the axe was laid at the root of the tree invoking Isaiah's image of judgment against the unrepentant (Isa. 6).

   2. John also declared that God's winnowing fork was in His hand and that He would separate the righteous and the wicked as the grain is separated from the chaff.

   3. John sounded the alarm that God's kingdom was near and its establishment would mean the redemption of the repentant and the judgment of the wicked.

G. John issued a call for repentance and baptism in the Jordan River.
   1. Faithful Israelites demonstrated their allegiance to the covenant through circumcision.

   2. Gentiles who wanted to join the covenant community were required to make a profession of faith, undergo the rite of circumcision, and be baptized.

   3. John as a Jewish prophet called for his Jewish listeners to be baptized and cleansed from their sins as common Gentiles.

   4. The Jewish authorities protested that they had Abraham as their father and did not need to be cleansed through baptism.

   5. Jewish commoners submitted to baptism and repented of their sins.

H. "And this is the testimony of John, when the Jews sent priests and Levites from Jerusalem to ask him, 'Who are you?' He confessed, and did not deny, but confessed, 'I am not the Christ.' And they asked him, 'What then? Are you Elijah?' He said, 'I am not.' 'Are you the Prophet?' And he answered, 'No.' So they said to him, 'Who are you? We need to give an answer to those who sent us. What do you say about yourself?' He said, 'I am the voice of one crying out in the wilderness, "Make straight the way of the Lord," as the prophet Isaiah said'" (John 1:19–28).

1. John is asked by the authorities if he is Elijah and he says he is not.

2. "And the disciples asked him, 'Then why do the scribes say that first Elijah must come?' He answered, 'Elijah does come, and he will restore all things. But I tell you that Elijah has already come, and they did not recognize him, but did to him whatever they pleased. So also the Son of Man will certainly suffer at their hands'" (Matt. 17:10–12).

3. According to Jesus the prophet Elijah came in the person of John the Baptist.

4. John the Baptist fulfilled the prophecy of the coming of Elijah.

5. "But the angel said to him, 'Do not be afraid, Zechariah, for your prayer has been heard, and your wife Elizabeth will bear you a son, and you shall call his name John. And you will have joy and gladness, and many will rejoice at his birth, for he will be great before the Lord. And he must not drink wine or strong drink, and he will be filled with the Holy Spirit, even from his mother's womb'" (Luke 1:13–15).

6. John the Baptist leaped in Elizabeth's womb when she met Mary thus giving witness to Christ even before his birth.

7. "And he will turn many of the children of Israel to the Lord their God, and he will go before him in the spirit and power of Elijah, to turn the hearts of the fathers to the children, and the disobedient to the wisdom of the just, to make ready for the Lord a people prepared" (Luke 1:16–17).

8. Elijah's prophetic ministry was revived in the mission of John the Baptist.

I. The most important aspect of John's mission was to bear witness to Jesus the Messiah.
1. Jesus had John baptize Him despite his reluctance.

2. Jesus had no sin of His own, but submitted to John's baptism in order to fulfill all aspects of the law.

3. John played a very significant role in the history of redemption.

BIBLE STUDY

1. Read Matthew 3:2. What are the two key parts of John the Baptist's message?

2. In Matthew 3:3, John the Baptist quotes Isaiah 40:3, which is part of a prophecy of future restoration in which Isaiah portrays the coming salvation of Israel in terms of a new exodus. By quoting this passage, what is John saying about the coming of Christ?

3. Compare Matthew 3:4 and 2 Kings 1:8. Who does John resemble in his style of clothing? How is this important in light of Malachi 4:5–6?

4. Compare Luke 3:3 with Acts 19:5. Is John's baptism identical to Christian baptism?

5. Read Luke 3:7–14. What is John's warning to those who fail to repent?

DISCUSSION

1. As we have seen, Malachi 4:5–6 prophesied that Elijah would come before the day of the Lord. John dressed like Elijah (Matt. 3:4), but was he Elijah? Read Jesus' statement in Matthew 11:14 and compare it to John's statement in John 1:21. How does Luke 1:17 help us to reconcile these statements?

2. When we recall the historical context of John's ministry—centuries of prophetic silence—how would first-century Jews view his ministry? What might they see as the significance of his words and work? How did John understand his own ministry?

3. In the Old Testament era, several prophets looked forward to a future outpouring of the Spirit. The prophecy of Joel 2:28–32 is particularly significant in this respect. What did John teach regarding the fulfillment of these prophecies (see Matt. 3:11)? How was his ministry related to the fulfillment of these prophecies?

FOR FURTHER STUDY

Keener, Craig. *A Commentary on the Gospel of Matthew*
France, R.T. *The Gospel of Mark*
Morris, Leon. *The Gospel According to John*
Sproul, R.C. *A Walk with God: An Exposition of Luke*
Sproul, R.C. *John* (St. Andrew's Expositional Commentary)
Stein, Robert H. *Luke*

33

The Birth of Jesus

MESSAGE INTRODUCTION

It was a great shock to many that God sent His son as one born of a virgin peasant girl outside of Jerusalem. Many were expecting the Messiah to be a great military or royal figure. However Jesus came not only to die, but also to live. His life began in very humble circumstances when an angel of the Lord came to a poor Jewish teenager and informed her that she would bear the Son of God. This was the beginning of the humiliation of Christ. A life that descended from glory was lived in service and sacrifice to restore many to glory. In this lecture, Dr. Sproul discusses the birth of Jesus.

SCRIPTURE READING

Matthew 1–2; Luke 1–2:20; John 1

LEARNING OBJECTIVES

1.   To emphasize the identity and mission of Christ as the second Adam.

2.   To highlight the role of miracles in the birth and life of Jesus.

3.   To identify the role of the Holy Spirit in the divine conception of Christ.

QUOTATIONS

Have this mind among yourselves, which is yours in Christ Jesus, who, though he was in the form of God, did not count equality with God a thing to be grasped, but made himself nothing, taking the form of a servant, being born in the likeness of men. And being found in human form, he humbled himself by becoming obedient to the point of death, even death on a cross. Therefore God has highly exalted him and bestowed on him the name that is above every name, so that at the name of Jesus every knee should bow, in heaven and on earth and under the earth, and every tongue confess that Jesus Christ is Lord, to the glory of God the Father.

—Philippians 2:5–11

LECTURE OUTLINE

A. It was a great shock to many that God sent His son as one born of a virgin peasant girl outside of Jerusalem.
- Many were expecting the Messiah to be a great military or royal figure.

B. Jesus came not only to die, but also to live. He came to be the second Adam.
1. The second Adam would accomplish what the first Adam failed to accomplish.

2. Jesus' mission was to be in submission to all the requirements of God.

3. Jesus took on a human nature and was born the son of a woman and as a son of David.

4. Jesus grew in favor with God and man, learned obedience, and expanded His understanding of His mission.

C. The birth of Jesus begins the humiliation of Christ.
1. The One who was equal with God did not jealously guard His position, but rather emptied Himself to take the position of a servant.

2. To accomplish His glorious ascent to heaven, Christ first had to experience His descent to earth.

D. "In the sixth month the angel Gabriel was sent from God to a city of Galilee named Nazareth, to a virgin betrothed to a man whose name was Joseph, of the house of David. And the virgin's name was Mary. And he came to her and said, 'Greetings, O favored one, the Lord is with you!' But she was greatly troubled at the saying, and tried to discern what sort of greeting this might be" (Luke 1:26–29).
1. Mary has been chosen by God for a profound and special blessing.

2. She is troubled because she is surprised by the visit of an angel of God.

E. "And the angel said to her, 'Do not be afraid, Mary, for you have found favor with God. And behold, you will conceive in your womb and bear a son, and you shall call his name Jesus. He will be great and will be called the Son of the Most High. And the Lord God will give to him the throne of his father David, and he will reign over the house of Jacob forever, and of his kingdom there will be no end'" (Luke 1:30–33).

   1. The Magnificat seems to show that Mary had an extensive understanding of the Old Testament prophecies regarding the coming Messiah.

   2. At the very least Mary understood she would become the mother of a king.

   3. Most likely Mary understood she was going to give birth to the Messiah who would restore the throne of David and defeat Israel's enemies.

F. "And Mary said to the angel, 'How will this be, since I am a virgin?'" (Luke 1:34).

   • Mary wondered how she would have a baby if she was not sexually active with a man.

G. "Now the birth of Jesus Christ took place in this way. When his mother Mary had been betrothed to Joseph, before they came together she was found to be with child from the Holy Spirit. And her husband Joseph, being a just man and unwilling to put her to shame, resolved to divorce her quietly" (Matt. 1:18–19).

   • Mary's pregnancy is an apparent embarrassment to Joseph, so he resolves to end the betrothal privately.

H. "But as he considered these things, behold, an angel of the Lord appeared to him in a dream, saying, 'Joseph, son of David, do not fear to take Mary as your wife, for that which is conceived in her is from the Holy Spirit. She will bear a son, and you shall call his name Jesus, for he will save his people from their sins'" (Matt. 1:20–21).

   • Matthew's gospel is quick to connect the birth of Jesus with Isaiah's prophecy of a virgin bearing a child named Immanuel.

I. The testimony of Scripture is clear that the circumstances surrounding Jesus' birth were miraculous.

   1. The virgin birth of Christ has been attacked by many who refuse to believe the Scriptural account.

   2. The life of Jesus is ablaze with miracles. His earthly life begins and ends with a miracle.

   3. Nineteenth-century liberalism advanced scholarship that de-mythologized the supernatural career of Jesus and cast Him into a human figure.

J. The virgin herself was the first one to struggle with believing in the virgin birth:
    *   "And the angel answered her, 'The Holy Spirit will come upon you, and the power of the Most High will overshadow you; therefore the child to be born will be called holy—the Son of God. And behold, your relative Elizabeth in her old age has also conceived a son, and this is the sixth month with her who was called barren. For nothing will be impossible with God'" (Luke 1:35–37).

K. The angel reassures Mary by telling her the child will be conceived within her by the power of the Holy Ghost.
    1. The word structure here is very similar to the opening verses of the creation account in Genesis 1.

    2. The Spirit hovered like a bird over the primordial waters to bring forth life upon the opening of creation.

    3. The Spirit will overshadow the virgin to bring forth life in her womb.

    4. The angel points Mary to Elizabeth as an example of God's supernatural power over the womb.

L. The New Testament emphasizes what is impossible with man is possible with God.
    1. It was not impossible for a virgin to bear a child through the power of God.

    2. It was impossible for the grave to hold the sinless Son of God.

M. "And Mary said, 'Behold, I am the servant of the Lord; let it be to me according to your word.' And the angel departed from her" (Luke 1:38).
    1. Mary's statement is sometimes called Mary's fiat or command to the angel to bring about the conception.

    2. St. Thomas Aquinas understood this statement to mean Mary's surrender to the will of God.

    3. Despite her fear, Mary's will is surrendered to God's plan.

N. "In those days a decree went out from Caesar Augustus that all the world should be registered" (Luke 2:1).
    1. God utilizes the decree of the most powerful man on earth to sovereignly accomplish the birth of His Son.

    2. Jesus is born in Bethlehem in fulfillment of Micah's prophecy regarding the birthplace of the Messiah.

BIBLE STUDY

1. Matthew's gospel begins with the statement: "The book of the genealogy of Jesus Christ, the son of David, the son of Abraham" (1:1). How does this statement connect the birth of Jesus to the promises of the Old Testament?

2. Read Isaiah 7:14. What does Isaiah prophesy here? Compare Isaiah's prophecy to the statement of its fulfillment in Matthew 1:21–23. Since "Immanuel" means "God with us," what does this say about the significance of Jesus' birth?

3. Read and compare the announcements of John the Baptist's birth in Luke 1:13–17 and Jesus' birth in Luke 1:30–33. What are the similarities and differences? In particular, what difference is evident when you compare verse 15 and verse 32?

4. In light of the many Old Testament prophecies concerning the coming restoration of Israel, what is the significance of the announcement in Luke 1:32?

5. Read Luke 2:1–7. How did God providentially oversee the fulfillment of Micah 5:2 in these events?

DISCUSSION

1. In the nineteenth century, many liberals rejected the doctrine of the virgin birth (or more properly, the virgin conception). How is the acceptance of this doctrine intimately connected to one's view of biblical authority? How is the acceptance of this doctrine intimately connected to one's view of miracles? How are the two related?

2. Some reject the doctrine of the virgin birth, saying that Jesus could not be fully human if He had only one human parent. How would you respond to this objection? Are Adam and Eve relevant to the discussion? If so, how?

3. What are some of the differences between the way the birth of Jesus is handled in the gospel narratives and the way it is handled in contemporary concepts of Christmas?

FOR FURTHER STUDY

Keener, Craig. *A Commentary on the Gospel of Matthew*
France, R.T. *The Gospel of Mark*
Sproul, R.C. *A Walk with God: An Exposition of Luke*
Sproul, R.C. *John* (St. Andrew's Expositional Commentary)
Stein, Robert H. *Luke*
Morris, Leon. *The Gospel According to John*

34

The Early Years of Jesus' Life

MESSAGE INTRODUCTION

Little is known regarding the early years of Jesus, but what the Scriptures make clear is that from birth Jesus was a very unique child. The birth of Christ caused many to break out in song as they rejoiced upon the arrival of the Messiah. Mary sang the Magnificat celebrating God's rescue of the lowly and His humbling of the mighty. Simeon willingly faced death, content in the fact that he had seen the Christ. Jesus' visit to the temple at the age of twelve made it clear even to His parents that their son was born to fulfill the messianic mission. In this lecture, Dr. Sproul discusses the early years of Jesus' life.

SCRIPTURE READING

Luke 1–2

LEARNING OBJECTIVES

1. To describe the major characteristics of the gospel genre.

2. To explain the significance of the Magnificat.

3. To explain the fulfillment of Simeon's prophecy.

QUOTATIONS

Long before Jesus began his public ministry, Luke revealed that he was aware of his unique relationship to God. Already at the age of twelve he knew that he was God's Son and that he possessed a unique calling.

—Robert Stein

LECTURE OUTLINE

A. God has given us four gospels or four accounts of the life of Christ in Scripture.

B. Matthew, Mark, and Luke are known as the Synoptic Gospels.
   - John is a non-Synoptic gospel.

C. The Synoptic Gospels offer the reader an overview or "synopsis" of the life of Christ.
   1. John's gospel focuses on Jesus' teaching and primarily on the week of His passion.

   2. The Gospels are not complete biographies of Christ.

   3. There is little information in the Gospels regarding the childhood of Jesus.

   4. Luke's account of Jesus' visit to the temple at the age of twelve is the only event recorded between Christ's infancy and His ministry.

D. The Gnostic gospels written in the second century included spurious accounts of Jesus as a child to fill in the details from these lost years.
   1. Jesus creates live birds from the mud in one of the Gnostic gospels.

   2. The church rejected the credibility and orthodoxy of the Gnostic gospels at an early date.

E. Luke extensively researched his material in the writing of his gospel.
   - Tradition suggests Luke interviewed Mary for the composition of his gospel which explains her prominent role in the gospel of Luke.

F. Songs play a prominent role in Luke's gospel including the Song of Zechariah, the Magnificat of Mary, and the Song of Simeon.
   1. Songs play a significant role in the Old Testament including the Song of Moses, the Song of Miriam, and the Song of Deborah.

   2. Military victories or festival celebrations were often occasions for the com position of a song.

   3. The celebration surrounding the birth of Jesus inspires several songs.

   4. God's people will sing a new song on the day of victory according to the book of Revelation (Rev. 5:9–10).

G. There are more stories of Jesus' encounters with women in the gospel of Luke than in all the other Gospels combined.

H. "And Mary said, 'My soul magnifies the Lord, and my spirit rejoices in God my Savior, for he has looked on the humble estate of his servant. For behold, from now on all generations will call me blessed'" (Luke 1:46–48).

1. The motif of the humble and shunned servant girl who is transformed is also present in the Magnificat.

2. Mary deeply rejoices because she has been noticed or regarded by God in her lowly estate.

3. All who receive the mercy of God have been noticed by the Prince and are raised up from their lowly estate.

I. "For he who is mighty has done great things for me, and holy is his name. And his mercy is for those who fear him from generation to generation. He has shown strength with his arm; he has scattered the proud in the thoughts of their hearts; he has brought down the mighty from their thrones and exalted those of humble estate" (Luke 1:49–52).

1. Mary envisions the rulers of this world reigning with arrogance and oppression in the face of the powerful majesty of God.

2. God looks with judgment upon the rulers of this world and pulls them down from their seats of power.

J. "He has filled the hungry with good things, and the rich he has sent empty away. He has helped his servant Israel, in remembrance of his mercy, as he spoke to our fathers, to Abraham and to his offspring forever" (Luke 1:53–55).

• Mary understands the birth of her child to be the fulfillment of promises made to Abraham.

K. "Now there was a man in Jerusalem, whose name was Simeon, and this man was righteous and devout, waiting for the consolation of Israel, and the Holy Spirit was upon him" (Luke 2:25).

1. "The Consolation of Israel" was one of the titles of the Messiah.

2. Isaiah had issued the prophetic call of, "Comfort, comfort my people" (Isa. 40:1).

L. "And it had been revealed to him by the Holy Spirit that he would not see death before he had seen the Lord's Christ. And he came in the Spirit into the temple, and when the parents brought in the child Jesus, to do for him according to the custom of the law, he took him up in his arms and blessed God and said, 'Lord, now you are letting your servant depart in peace, according to your word; for my eyes have seen your salvation that you have prepared in the presence of all peoples, a light for revelation to the Gentiles, and for glory to your people Israel'" (Luke 2:26–32).

1. Simeon recognizes Jesus as the consolation of Israel and therefore the Messiah.

2. Jesus was brought to the temple to be circumcised, named, and as the first-born He was dedicated to God.

3. The offering of two birds that Joseph and Mary give at the temple indicates their deep poverty.

4. Simeon can die in peace now that he has seen the Messiah.

M. "And his father and his mother marveled at what was said about him. And Simeon blessed them and said to Mary his mother, 'Behold, this child is appointed for the fall and rising of many in Israel, and for a sign that is opposed (and a sword will pierce through your own soul also), so that thoughts from many hearts may be revealed'" (Luke 2:33–35).

1. Luke probably interviewed Mary in order to write his gospel account.

2. Mary most likely remembered this prophecy from Simeon about her heart being pierced as she stood at the foot of the cross.

N. The prophetess, Anna, also greeted Jesus' parents and spoke about Jesus to many at the temple.

O. "Now his parents went to Jerusalem every year at the Feast of the Passover. And when he was twelve years old, they went up according to custom. And when the feast was ended, as they were returning, the boy Jesus stayed behind in Jerusalem. His parents did not know it, but supposing him to be in the group they went a day's journey, but then they began to search for him among their relatives and acquaintances" (Luke 2:41–44).

1. Families traveling to Jerusalem often traveled in caravans with the men separate from the women.

2. Joseph probably assumed his son was with Mary and she assumed Jesus was with Joseph.

3. Joseph and Mary discover they accidentally left their son back in Jerusalem.

P. "And when they did not find him, they returned to Jerusalem, searching for him. After three days they found him in the temple, sitting among the teachers, listening to them and asking them questions. And all who heard him were amazed at his understanding and his answers. And when his parents saw him they were astonished. And his mother said to him, 'Son, why have you treated us so? Behold, your father and I have been searching for you in great distress'" (Luke 2:45–48).
   1. Jesus was sinless, but Mary questions His obedience here.

Q. "And he said to them, 'Why were you looking for me? Did you not know that I must be in my Father's house?'" (Luke 2:49).
   1. From an early age Jesus was keenly aware of His messianic mission.

   2. The remainder of the Gospels reveals the story of Jesus' mission.

BIBLE STUDY

1. Read Mary's song (the Magnificat) in Luke 1:46–55. In what ways does Mary speak as the representative of Israel? How does Mary describe God in this song? How is Mary's song similar to the Song of Hannah in 1 Samuel 2:1–10?

2. After the birth of John the Baptist, we read Zechariah's benediction in Luke 1:67–79. How does Zechariah tie the redemptive roles of John and Jesus together here? According to Zechariah, who is Jesus?

3. Read the account of the angel's announcement to the shepherds on the night of Jesus' birth. How does the angel of the Lord identify the newborn child in verse 11?

4. When Jesus is brought to the temple, a man named Simeon takes the child up in his arms, blesses the child, and then the parents (see Luke 2:25–35). What does Simeon say about Jesus in his blessing of Him? What does he say in his blessing of the parents, and how do his words compare to Isaiah 8:14–15?

5. Read the account of Jesus at the temple in Luke 2:41–51. What is revealed in this story about Jesus' awareness of His mission? How is Jesus' uniqueness revealed to those around Him even at this young age of twelve?

DISCUSSION

1. In modern biographies, authors spend a lot of time talking about the childhood of their subject. Why do the authors of the Gospels say so little about Jesus' childhood?

2. In Luke 2:52, we read that Jesus "increased in wisdom and in stature and in favor with God and man." In 1 Samuel 2:26, similar language is used to describe Samuel, and in Proverbs 3:4 similar language is used to describe a son who follows the instruction of father. What, then, is this text in Luke telling us about Jesus in His human nature?

3. In the ancient world, women were not given a place of prominence. How do the first two chapters of Luke emphasize the role of women in the early years of Jesus' life? Why is this important?

FOR FURTHER STUDY

Keener, Craig. *A Commentary on the Gospel of Matthew*
France, R.T. *The Gospel of Mark*
Sproul, R.C. *A Walk with God: An Exposition of Luke*
Stein, Robert H. *Luke*

35

The Baptism
and Temptation of Jesus

MESSAGE INTRODUCTION

Scripture records three occasions in which the voice of God spoke from heaven pronouncing Jesus as the Son of God. The first pronouncement occurred at Jesus' baptism, which was also the moment that Jesus was anointed by the Spirit and commissioned as the Messiah. Immediately after His baptism, the same Spirit led Him into the wilderness to be tempted by Satan. In the desolate barrenness of the Judean wilderness, Jesus endured the full assault of Satan against His identity as the Son of God. His Father's pronouncement would be of paramount importance as Jesus did battle with the Evil One with the Word of God hanging in the balance. In this lecture, Dr. Sproul discusses the baptism and temptation of Jesus.

SCRIPTURE READING

Matthew 3:13–4:11; Mark 1; Luke 4:1–13; John 1

LEARNING OBJECTIVES

1. To discuss the second Adam motif of the New Testament.

2. To discuss the relationship between temptation and the integrity of God's Word.

3. To describe the wilderness temptations of Christ.

QUOTATIONS

For we do not have a high priest who is unable to sympathize with our weaknesses, but one who in every respect has been tempted as we are, yet without sin. Let us then with confidence draw near to the throne of grace, that we may receive mercy and find grace to help in time of need.

—Hebrews 4:15–16

LECTURE OUTLINE

A. The Gospels do not give any information regarding Jesus' life between the ages of twelve and thirty.

B. Jesus presumably grew up with Joseph and Mary and learned the trade of a carpenter.
   1. Jesus frequently used agricultural images in His teaching, but He most frequently used images related to stonemasonry.

   2. First century carpenters were builders who worked more with stone than wood.

   3. Jesus was probably quite strong and muscular because of His trade.

C. Jesus willingly submitted to every element of the law of God during His life including the rite of baptism.
   1. The Holy Spirit descended as a dove upon Christ at His baptism as a symbol of His ordination or divine commissioning.

   2. God spoke audibly from heaven and declared Jesus to be His Son at His baptism.

   3. The same Spirit that anointed Jesus at His baptism drove Him into the wilderness to be tempted by Satan for forty days.

D. An important motif of the New Testament is that Jesus, the second Adam, will succeed where the first Adam failed.
   • Jesus experienced a period of testing in the Judean wilderness before the commencement of His public ministry.

E. The Judean wilderness was a very desolate, dry, and rocky territory with only a few rabbits, snakes, scorpions, and birds.

- Jesus was driven by the Spirit into this territory to be alone for His period of temptation and trial.

F. Adam underwent his time of testing in a gorgeous and lush paradise with the freedom to eat from all the trees except one.
   - Jesus underwent his time of testing in a desolate wilderness amid a forty day fast.

G. Adam had the support of Eve during his testing, but Jesus was all alone in the wilderness.

H. Satan's point of attack against Eve was to raise questions regarding the veracity and trustworthiness of the Word of God.

I. "And the tempter came and said to him. 'If you are the Son of God, command these stones to become loaves of bread'" (Matt. 4:3).
   1. Satan's point of attack against Jesus in the wilderness was against the words of God at His baptism, "This is my Son in whom I am well pleased."

   2. Jesus understood the words of the devil as an attack against the Word of God and therefore responded with the Word of God.

   3. "But he answered, 'It is written, "Man shall not live by bread alone, but by every word that comes from the mouth of God"'" (Matt. 4:4).

   4. Jesus, the second Adam, would succeed where the first Adam failed by obeying every Word that proceeded from the mouth of God.

J. "And the devil took him up and showed him all the kingdoms of the world in a moment of time, and said to him, 'To you I will give all this authority and their glory, for it has been delivered to me, and I give it to whom I will. If you, then, will worship me, it will all be yours.' And Jesus answered him, 'It is written, "You shall worship the Lord your God, and him only shall you serve"'" (Luke 4:5–8).
   1. Satan offered Jesus the kingdoms of this world without the suffering of the cross.

   2. Jesus rebuked Peter later for suggesting any course of action that led away from the cross and its suffering.

K. "And he took him to Jerusalem and set him on the pinnacle of the temple and said to him, 'If you are the Son of God, throw yourself down from here, for it is written, "He will command his angels concerning you, to guard you," and "On their hands they will bear you up, lest you strike your foot against a stone"'" (Luke 4:9–11).
   • Satan quoted Scripture in order to continue his attack against the Word of God.

L. Jesus demonstrated that one portion of Scripture must not be set against another portion of Scripture.
   1. Scripture is the most important interpreter of Scripture.

   2. "And Jesus answered him, 'It is said, 'You shall not put the Lord your God to the test'" (Luke 4:12).

M. "And when the devil had ended every temptation, he departed from him until an opportune time" (Luke 4:13).
   1. Satan departed and the angels of God ministered to Jesus in the wilderness.

   2. God's Word is shown to be true in that He does guard the righteous with His angels.

BIBLE STUDY

1. Read the account of Jesus' baptism in Matthew 3:13–17. How does the prophecy of Isaiah 11:1–9 begin to be fulfilled in the baptism of Jesus? Compare the language of Matthew 3:17 and Isaiah 42:1. If Matthew's words echo Isaiah's words, what does that say about Jesus?

2. Compare the temptation of Jesus in Matthew 4:1–11 with the temptation of Adam and Eve in Genesis 3. What are the similarities and differences between the two?

3. Who led Jesus into the wilderness to be tempted (Matt. 4:1)? Why might this be significant?

4. Read Matthew 4:3 and 4:6. What is Satan attempting to get Jesus to doubt? What did God say in Matthew 3:17?

5. What is the same in all three of Jesus' responses to Satan in Matthew 4:4, 7, and 10? To what does Jesus appeal in order to overcome Satan's temptations?

DISCUSSION

1. In Matthew 4:8–9, Satan offers to give Jesus all of the kingdoms of the world if Jesus will fall down and worship him. Were these kingdoms Satan's to give? What do the following passages contribute to the discussion: John 12:31; 14:30; 2 Corinthians 4:4?

2. Matthew seems to draw a number of parallels in the early chapters of his gospel between the life of Christ and the early history of Israel. The baptism and temptation of Jesus, for example, echo in some ways the events of the exodus and wilderness wandering. If these parallels are real, what is Matthew attempting to teach us about Jesus?

3. What are the similarities and differences, if any, between John's baptism and Christian baptism? How would such similarities and/or differences influence our understanding of the practice of Christian baptism?

FOR FURTHER STUDY

Keener, Craig. *A Commentary on the Gospel of Matthew*
France, R.T. *The Gospel of Mark*
Sproul, R.C. *A Walk with God: An Exposition of Luke*
Sproul, R.C. *John* (St. Andrew's Expositional Commentary)
Stein, Robert H. *Luke*
Morris, Leon. *The Gospel According to John*

36

Jesus' Inaugural Address and Public Ministry

MESSAGE INTRODUCTION

Jesus' call on His disciples to follow Him was much more extraordinary than may at first appear. Jesus lived His life as an itinerant rabbi traveling from place to place teaching in synagogues and in the outdoors. As His disciples traveled with Him they witnessed supernatural healings and listened to liberating teaching. Yet the life to which Jesus called them was neither glamorous nor rewarding according to what this world values. Therefore He pronounced His beatitudes or blessings upon those who weep, mourn, hunger, and are persecuted in this life. For the momentary trials they would endure in this life would be nothing compared to the glory they would be given in the kingdom to come. In this lecture, Dr. Sproul discusses Jesus' inaugural address and public ministry.

SCRIPTURE READING

Matthew 4:12–7; Luke 4:14–6; John 2–4

LEARNING OBJECTIVES

1. To describe Jesus' appropriation of the messianic mission.

2. To discuss the difference between an apostle and a disciple.

3. To describe Jesus' revolutionary teaching in the Beatitudes.

QUOTATIONS

The Beatitudes come like a bolt out of the blue for any who think of religion as a sad and miserable affair. Maybe "religion" is. But the kingdom of God is quite different. In participating, we are the way God meant us to be, and so it is inevitably the happy life. And that is what "blessed" means: made happy by God. It is as if Jesus is saying that life in the kingdom with him is a life of profound joy, a joy that no person and no circumstance can take away. And this blessedness is not reserved for some nebulous future. It is for now! It is the mark of those who have really surrendered to the King and tasted his grace, although of course there is a future to rejoice in too.

—Michael Green

LECTURE OUTLINE

A. Jesus is led into the wilderness by the Spirit to be tempted by the devil and then He returns to Galilee in the power of the Spirit.
   1. Jesus begins His public ministry with extraordinary teaching.

B. "And he came to Nazareth, where he had been brought up. And as was his custom, he went to the synagogue on the Sabbath day, and he stood up to read" (Luke 4:16).
   • Jesus functioned as an itinerant rabbi without a settled location to teach or sleep.

C. "And the scroll of the prophet Isaiah was given to him. He unrolled the scroll and found the place where it was written, 'The Spirit of the Lord is upon me, because he has anointed me to proclaim good news to the poor. He has sent me to proclaim liberty to the captives and recovering of sight to the blind, to set at liberty those who are oppressed, to proclaim the year of the Lord's favor'" (Luke 4:17–19).
   1. People sat on the floor in a synagogue in order to listen to a rabbi's teaching.

   2. The rabbi would sit on a chair or bench in order to explain the Hebrew text and the worshippers would sit at his feet.

   3. Jesus read the text from Isaiah and then sat in the posture of a teaching rabbi in order to explain the text.

D. "And he rolled up the scroll and gave it back to the attendant and sat down. And the eyes of all in the synagogue were fixed on him. And he began to say to them, 'Today this Scripture has been fulfilled in your hearing'" (Luke 4:20–21).
   • Isaiah 61 is the job description of the Messiah, and Jesus points to Himself as fulfilling that role.

E. "And he began to say to them, 'Today this Scripture has been fulfilled in your hearing.' And all spoke well of him and marveled at the gracious words that were coming from his mouth. And they said, 'Is not this Joseph's son?' And he said to them, 'Doubtless you will quote to me this proverb, "Physician, heal yourself." What we have heard you did at Capernaum, do here in your hometown as well.' And he said, 'Truly, I say to you, no prophet is acceptable in his hometown'" (Luke 4:21–24).
   •   This is a dramatic moment in Jesus' life because He identifies Himself with the Messiah's mission.

F. Jesus selected His disciples at the beginning of His Galilean ministry after spending a complete night in prayer.
    1. A disciple and an apostle are not the same office in the New Testament.

    2. Jesus chose many disciples or "learners" to follow Him in His teachings and travels.

    3. From His disciples He chose a select group of twelve to be His apostles or representatives that would speak for Him.

    4. An apostle has the authority of an ambassador representing a greater sovereign in order to speak or negotiate in his name.

G. "And he went throughout all Galilee, teaching in their synagogues and proclaiming the gospel of the kingdom and healing every disease and every affliction among the people. So his fame spread throughout all Syria, and they brought him all the sick, those afflicted with various diseases and pains, those oppressed by demons, epileptics, and paralytics, and he healed them. And great crowds followed him from Galilee and the Decapolis, and from Jerusalem and Judea, and from beyond the Jordan" (Matt. 4:23–25).
    1. This is the setting Matthew gives immediately before Jesus preaches the Sermon on the Mount.

    2. Jesus preaches the Sermon after He has identified Himself as the One who is anointed to bring comfort to those who mourn, freedom to those held captive, and healing to the diseased and broken.

H. "Seeing the crowds, he went up on the mountain, and when he sat down, his disciples came to him. And he opened his mouth and taught them, saying: 'Blessed are the poor in spirit, for theirs is the kingdom of heaven'" (Matt. 5:1–3).
    1. The Old Testament prophets delivered their messages through oracles of weal and woe.

2. Jesus adopts the form of a weal oracle to deliver statements regarding God's blessing or beatitudes.

3. Jesus speaks not of a superficial happiness, but rather a joy found deep in the soul.

4. Jesus turns the platitudes of this world upside down by celebrating those who mourn, the poor, the meek, the hungry, the merciful, the pure in heart, the peacemakers, and the persecuted.

5. Jesus as the Messiah is pronouncing the fulfillment of God's promise to comfort His people as prophesied in Isaiah 40.

I. For each pronouncement of blessedness He attaches a promise for the future.
   • The prerequisites for blessedness run in dramatic contradiction to this world's values.

J. "Blessed are those who are persecuted for righteousness' sake, for theirs is the kingdom of heaven. Blessed are you when others revile you and persecute you and utter all kinds of evil against you falsely on my account. Rejoice and be glad, for your reward is great in heaven, for so they persecuted the prophets who were before you" (Matt. 5:10–12).
   1. The trend of nineteenth-century liberalism was to remove the supernatural and miraculous elements from the life of Christ.

   2. Jesus was portrayed strictly as a great ethical, yet human, teacher.

K. The One who preached the Sermon on the Mount is not just sharing His wisdom, but is also declaring who will inherit the kingdom of God and who will not.
   1. He pronounces a blessing upon those who are persecuted for the sake of His name.

   2. Jesus is not just sharing facts in the Sermon, but is also revealing Himself and the kingdom He will establish.

L. "Not everyone who says to me, 'Lord, Lord,' will enter the kingdom of heaven, but the one who does the will of my Father who is in heaven. On that day many will say to me, 'Lord, Lord, did we not prophesy in your name, and cast out demons in your name, and do many mighty works in your name?' And then will I declare to them, 'I never knew you; depart from me, you workers of lawlessness'" (Matt. 7:21–23).
   1. This warning of exclusion is the climax of the Sermon on the Mount.

2. Many on the last day will feign intimacy with Jesus and claim they accomplished much for Him.

3. Jesus will declare that He never knew them and cast them away.

M. The ultimate test for citizenship in Jesus' kingdom will not be if you know Jesus, but rather, *does He know you?*

BIBLE STUDY

1. In Luke 4:14–30, which describes Jesus' rejection in Nazareth, Jesus reads from Isaiah 61:1–2 while in the synagogue. The prophecy in Isaiah speaks of the salvation that the Messiah will bring in terms of the Jubilee (Leviticus 25:1–12). What is Jesus saying to the people of Nazareth in His reading of this Isaiah prophecy?

2. Read the account of Jesus' early Galilean ministry in Matthew 4:23–24. How might the actions of Jesus described here indicate a foretaste of the coming of the kingdom? How might these events indicate a foretaste of the reversal of the curse that fell upon mankind at the time of the Fall in Eden?

3. In Matthew 5:17, Jesus says that He has come to fulfill the law and the Prophets. Read Matthew 11:13. According to this verse, what did the law and the Prophets do "until John"? Does this shed any light on how we understand the meaning of "fulfill" in 5:17? How do these verses underscore the fact that everything the Old Testament foreshadowed and symbolized became a reality in Christ?

4. Read Jesus' words on anger, lust, divorce, oaths, retaliation, and the love of one's enemies in Matthew 5:21–48. What does each announcement have in common? What does this commonality say about the authority of Jesus?

5. In Matthew 6:1–18, Jesus instructs his hearers on the subjects of giving, prayer, and fasting. What do his instructions on each of these three topics have in common?

DISCUSSION

1. In Matthew 6:25–34, Jesus speaks to His disciples on the subject of anxiety and worry. He tells them that they should not worry about food or clothing because God will provide. Are Jesus' words a blanket condemnation of all worry and/or anxiety? Are there any examples of "godly" anxiety in Scripture? In the life of Jesus? Does it depend on how we define anxiety?

2. What does it mean for Christ's disciples to seek first the kingdom of God (Matt. 6:33)?

3. Jesus warns His disciples about judging in Matthew 7:1–5. What three reasons does Jesus give to explain why we should not judge? How has this text been abused in our day?

FOR FURTHER STUDY

Carson, D.A. *Jesus' Sermon on the Mount and His Confrontation with the World*
Keener, Craig. *A Commentary on the Gospel of Matthew*
Ferguson, Sinclair. *The Sermon on the Mount*
France, R.T. *The Gospel of Mark*
Sproul, R.C. *A Walk with God: An Exposition of Luke*
Stein, Robert H. *Luke*

The Teaching of Jesus: Parables

MESSAGE INTRODUCTION

The teaching of Jesus was considered extraordinary in His day because He spoke with authority. Even those who reject Christ as Lord and Savior today still hold His teaching in high regard. Profound content was made clear with illustrations and the parable was His favorite form of illustration. He used parables as riddles to trap His opponents or simple tales to encourage His disciples. His teaching revealed the mysteries of the kingdom to His followers and concealed its glory from the hard hearted. In this lecture, Dr. Sproul discusses the teaching of Jesus.

SCRIPTURE READING

Matthew 10–12; Mark 2–3; Luke 10–15

LEARNING OBJECTIVES

1. To explain how Jesus taught with authority.

2. To define the literary device of the parable.

3. To identify important principles in interpreting parables.

QUOTATIONS

The parable form comes through in the Old Testament and was part of the teaching repertoire of the Jewish sages. So, by using the parable form, Jesus claims to be a teacher in the wisdom tradition of the Old Testament. We are to sit at His feet and listen to His authoritative teaching.

The parable suited Jesus' purpose for other reasons. It offered glimpses of realities that people were not prepared to understand in their entirety. Parables both revealed truths about the kingdom of God and at the same time shrouded it in mystery. The parable was the ideal teaching vehicle for subjects beyond human comprehension. Parables speak to us in a poetic language of picture images. The parables teach us about things we don't know by comparing them to things we do know in our everyday experience.

—Tremper Longman III

LECTURE OUTLINE

A. "When they heard these words, some of the people said, 'This really is the Prophet.' Others said, 'This is the Christ.' But some said, 'Is the Christ to come from Galilee? Has not the Scripture said that the Christ comes from the offspring of David, and comes from Bethlehem, the village where David was?' So there was a division among the people over him. Some of them wanted to arrest him, but no one laid hands on him. The officers then came to the chief priests and Pharisees, who said to them, 'Why did you not bring him?' The officers answered, 'No one ever spoke like this man!'" (John 7:40–46).

B. Jesus was known for being one who spoke and taught with authority.
   1. He did not speak lightly, but rather with substance.

   2. "So Jesus answered them, 'My teaching is not mine, but his who sent me. If anyone's will is to do God's will, he will know whether the teaching is from God or whether I am speaking on my own authority'" (John 7:16–17).

C. The content as well as the manner of Jesus' teaching was considered extraordinary.
   1. Even those who reject Jesus as Lord and Savior acknowledge Him as a master teacher.

   2. Jesus was particularly known for His parables.

D. Parables are rare in the Old Testament, frequent in the Synoptic Gospels, and entirely absent in the gospel of John and the rest of the New Testament.

E. Parables need to be distinguished from other figures of speech.
   1. Similes and metaphors offer a comparison between two things.

   2. A hyperbole is an intentional exaggeration to underscore or emphasize a certain point.

F. A literal translation of the word *parable* is "something thrown alongside something else."

G. The most important rule in interpreting a passage of Scripture is context, and a very important element in dynamic teaching is illustration.
    •   Jesus' principle form of illustration which He threw alongside His declarations of truth, were parables.

H. Jesus taught long parables such as the parable of the lost son and the parable of the good Samaritan," but also shorter ones such as the parable of the blind leading the blind.

I. Parables can often function as a riddle in situations of conflict in order to trap one's opponent in a debate.
    1. The Pharisees debated among themselves who was their neighbor and therefore who they were required to love.

    2. Jesus tells the parable of the good Samaritan in order to surprise the Pharisees in their thinking.

J. "And he said, 'He who has ears to hear, let him hear.' And when he was alone, those around him with the twelve said to them, 'To you has been given the secret of the kingdom of God, but for those outside everything is in parables, so that 'they may indeed see but not perceive, and my indeed hear but not understand, lest they should turn and be forgiven'''" (Mark 4:9–12).
    1. The parables served the dual purpose of concealing and revealing the secrets of the kingdom of God.

    2. As in the day of Isaiah God had visited His day of judgment against those who did not want to hear His Word and therefore it was concealed from them.

K. There are important principles to remember when interpreting a parable.

L. A parable is not normally an allegory.
    •   Every element in a parable does not represent something else.

M. Most parables are designed to present one single point.

N. Many parables demonstrate the "rule of three" such as the parable of the prodigal son with three characters and the parable of the good Samaritan with three men who encounter the robbed man.
    •   The "rule of two" is often employed to draw a contrast in a story such as the conflict between the elder son and the prodigal son.

O. A comparison using the phrase "how much more" is also often used in the parables.

- The judgment of the unjust judge is set in contrast to the judgment of Almighty God.

P. The primary motif of the parables is the kingdom of God.

BIBLE STUDY

1. Read the parable of the sower and the seeds in Mark 4:3–20. Is the focus of the parable on the sower, the seed, the soil, or the harvest?

2. Jesus tells a number of parables to reveal truths about the kingdom of God. Read each of the following short parables and name the one point about the kingdom that each reveals:

    - The Growing Seed   (Mark 4:26–29)
    - The Wheat and the Weeds   (Matthew 13:24–30)
    - The Mustard Seed   (Matthew 13:31–32)
    - The Leaven   (Matthew 13:33)
    - The Treasure   (Matthew 13:44)
    - The Pearl   (Matthew 13:45–46)

3. Read the parable of the good Samaritan in Luke 10:25–37. Keeping in mind that the Jews viewed Samaritans as half-breed, unclean people, what is the significance of Jesus' teaching in this story?

4. The parable of the barren fig tree is found in Luke 13:6–9. Does this parable shed any light on Jesus' words in Matthew 21:18–22? If so, what is it?

5. Read the parable of the Pharisee and the tax collector in Luke 18:9–14. What kind of prayer is Jesus warning us against?

DISCUSSION

1. In Mark 4:10–12, Jesus indicates that one of the reasons He uses parables is in order that some might not understand. Why does Jesus purposely conceal His teaching from some and not from others?

2. What relevance do the parables of the mustard seed and the leaven (Matt. 13:31–33) have for our eschatology—our understanding of the last things?

3. Read Deuteronomy 26:13–15. What is the difference between what God commands His people to do here and what the Pharisee does in the parable of the Pharisee and the tax collector (Luke 18:9–14)?

FOR FURTHER STUDY

Bailey, Kenneth E. *Poet and Peasant and Through Peasant Eyes*
Keener, Craig. *A Commentary on the Gospel of Matthew*
France, R.T. *The Gospel of Mark*
Sproul, R.C. *A Walk with God: An Exposition of Luke*
Stein, Robert H. *Luke*

38

Interpreting Parables

MESSAGE INTRODUCTION

An important aspect of the mission of Christ was to seek and save the lost. The lost He sought were the unrighteous, the outcasts, and the spiritually bankrupt. Reaching out to such sinners attracted the scorn of the Pharisees and the shocked looks of the self-righteous. Hoping to explain His heart for the lost, Jesus told a series of parables recorded in Luke 15 designed to convey the Father's joy when even a single sinner is found and restored. In this lecture, Dr. Sproul interprets the parables of Jesus recorded in Luke 15.

SCRIPTURE READING

Matthew 13; Mark 4; Luke 15–21

LEARNING OBJECTIVES

1. To defend the variety of themes and formats among the gospel writers.

2. To explain Jesus' purpose in telling the parables of Luke 15.

3. To highlight the central theme of the parables recorded in Luke 15.

QUOTATIONS

Jesus' parables often have an unexpected or surprise element in them. Most parables project a familiar world, but then introduce some radically unfamiliar element, something unexpected. It is this surprise element which provokes a hearer into a reexamination of his worldview, and thus which is the 'main point' of the parable.

—Dan McCartney and Charles Clayton

LECTURE OUTLINE

A. The parable of the prodigal son is grouped by Luke in his gospel with two other parables about something lost and then found.

B. The gospel writers will often arrange their material with different approaches, but the content is faithful to the original teachings of Jesus.
    1. Critics attack the text of the Gospels for repetitions and variant arrangements of the material.

    2. The gospel writers used various approaches to communicate their material including geographical, topical, and chronological formats.

    3. Modern writers and preachers also repeat important material in various formats and arrangements.

C. "Now the tax collectors and sinners were all drawing near to hear him. And the Pharisees and the scribes grumbled, saying, 'This man receives sinners and eats with them'" (Luke 15:1–2).
    1. The depraved and the outcasts flocked to Jesus' teaching, but the religious establishment condemned Him and His teaching.

    2. Jesus gives a series of parables to express His mission to the lost and unrighteous and His rebuke of the self-righteous Pharisees.

D. "So he told them this parable: 'What man of you, having a hundred sheep, if he has lost one of them, does not leave the ninety-nine in the open country, and go after the one that is lost, until he finds it? And when he has found it, he lays it on his shoulders, rejoicing. And when he comes home, he calls together his friends and his neighbors, saying to them, "Rejoice with me, for I have found my sheep that was lost." Just so, I tell you, there will be more joy in heaven over one sinner who repents than over ninety-nine righteous persons who need no repentance'" (Luke 15:3–7).
    1. Jesus actively sought out the lost and those in need and drew them to Himself and did not passively wait for them to come to Him.

    2. It is important that the church does not lose the part of its mission to go out and actively seek the lost.

E. "Or what woman, having ten silver coins, if she loses one coin, does not light a lamp and sweep the house and seek diligently until she finds it? And when she has found it, she calls together her friends and neighbors, saying, 'Rejoice with me, for I have found the coin that I had lost.' Just so, I tell you, there is joy before the angels of God over one sinner who repents" (Luke 15:8–10).

- Jesus reiterates His theme: when the lost are sought and found then it brings great rejoicing.

F. "And he said, 'There was a man who had two sons. And the younger of them said to his father, "Father, give me the share of property that is coming to me." And he divided his property between them. Not many days later, the younger son gathered all he had and took a journey into a far country, and there he squandered his property in reckless living'" (Luke 15:11–13).
  1. A "far country" is always the place we prefer to go to sin so that we do not ruin our reputation in front of those who know us.

  2. The son quickly wastes what it took years for the Father to earn.

G. "And when he had spent everything, a severe famine arose in that country, and he began to be in need. So he went and hired himself out to one of the citizens of that country, who sent him into his fields to feed pigs. And he was longing to be fed with the pods that the pigs ate, and no one gave him anything" (Luke 15:14–16).
  1. The son's degradation is especially poignant for a Jewish audience that considered the pig to be unclean.

  2. We often only seek the voice of God when we hit bottom.

  3. The prodigal's father had given him everything, but he despised the gifts of his father. Now no one will give him anything.

H. "But when he came to himself, he said, 'How many of my father's hired servants have more than enough bread, but I perish here with hunger!'" (Luke 15:17).
  1. Spiritual revivals have often been called "awakenings" as people have been roused from their sleep to the things of God.

  2. The son does not come to himself by himself, but rather is awakened by the Holy Spirit.

I. "But when he came to himself, he said, 'How many of my father's hired servants have more than enough bread, but I perish here with hunger! I will arise and go to my father, and I will say to him, "Father, I have sinned against heaven and before you. I am no longer worthy to be called your son. Treat me as one of your hired servants"'" (Luke 15:17–19).
  - The son acknowledges his sin and his unworthiness to even be his father's son.

J. "And he arose and came to his father. But while he was still a long way off, his father saw him and felt compassion, and ran and embraced him and kissed him" (Luke 15:20).

- The father does not stand back with a scowl and a condemning look, but rather runs to him.

K. "And the son said to him, 'Father, I have sinned against heaven and before you. I am no longer worthy to be called your son.' But the father said to his servants, 'Bring quickly the best robe, and put it on him, and put a ring on his hand, and shoes on his feet. And bring the fattened calf and kill it, and let us eat and celebrate. For this my son was dead, and is alive again; he was lost, and is found.' And they began to celebrate" (Luke 15:21–24).
  - The father gives the son everything the son does not deserve.

L. The Pharisees are represented by the older brother in the story.
  - "Meanwhile, the older son was in the fields working. When he returned home, he heard music and dancing in the house, and he asked one of the servants what was going on. 'Your brother is back.' he was told, 'and your father has killed the calf we were fattening and has prepared a great feast. We are celebrating because of his safe return.' The older brother was angry and wouldn't go in. His father came out and begged him, but he replied, 'All these years I've worked hard for you and never once refused to do a single thing you told me to. And in all that time you never gave me even one young goat for a feast with my friends. Yet when this son of yours comes back after squandering your money on prostitutes, you celebrate by killing the finest calf we have'" (Luke 15:25–30).

M. The father points the elder brother to the significance of his son's return and also highlights the self-righteousness of the Pharisees.
  1. "His father said to him, 'Look, dear son, you and I are very close, and everything I have is yours. We had to celebrate this happy day. For your brother was dead and has come back to life! He was lost, but now he is found!'" (Luke 15:31–32).

  2. Jesus told this parable to explain why He fellowshipped with sinners and to explain that He came to seek and save the lost.

BIBLE STUDY

1. The parables of Luke 15 are set within the context of Jesus' conflict with the Pharisees about associating with tax collectors and sinners. How do each of the three parables in Luke 15 contribute to the overarching theme of good news for outcasts?

2. Compare the parable of the lost sheep in Luke 15:4–7 with Ezekiel 34:4–24. What themes in Ezekiel does Jesus pick up on in His parable? What are the similarities and differences between Ezekiel 34 and Luke 15?

3. What are the points of similarity and dissimilarity between the parable of the lost sheep" (Luke 15:4–7) and the parable of the lost coin (Luke 15:8–10)? Do any of the differences have potential theological significance?

4. Read the parable of the prodigal son in Luke 15:11–32. Who is represented by the younger brother? The older brother? The father? How does this parable address the problem expressed in Luke 15:1–2?

5. What is the difference between the attitudes of the father and older brother respectively toward the younger brother's repentance? How does Jesus use this story to invite the Pharisees to adopt God's attitude toward the repentant?

DISCUSSION

1. Read the parable of the lost sheep in Matthew 18:12–14 and Luke 15:4–7. Many scholars note the differences between the two versions and devote considerable energy to figuring out which version is closer to the original parable as spoken by Jesus. Is there any reason to suppose, however, that Jesus could not tell similar stories over the course of his three-year teaching ministry?

2. In the parable of the lost sheep (Luke 15:4–7), what, if anything, is the significance of the 99 sheep who need no repentance? Is Jesus saying that there are humans who do not have any need to repent? Is He making a more subtle point about the difference between those who are obviously sinners and those who outwardly meet the standards of Scripture?

3. If the older brother in the parable of the prodigal son represents the Pharisees, why are the comments about the elder brother essentially positive? How does this help us to see that not every detail of a parable has theological significance?

FOR FURTHER STUDY

Bailey, Kenneth E. *Poet and Peasant and Through Peasant Eyes*
Keener, Craig. *A Commentary on the Gospel of Matthew*
France, R.T. *The Gospel of Mark*
Sproul, R.C. *A Walk with God: An Exposition of Luke*
Stein, Robert H. *Luke*

39

The Miracles of Jesus

MESSAGE INTRODUCTION

The New Testament is often rejected as authoritative and inspired because of its numerous accounts of miracles. Miracles often accompany a new revelation of God in the Scriptures, and therefore it is not surprising that many miracles accompanied God's greatest revelation in the person of Jesus Christ. Jesus appealed to His miracles as credentials of His Messiahship and signs that He was endorsed and blessed by God. The resurrection of Christ was the greatest miracle of all forever proving the identity of Jesus. In this lecture, Dr. Sproul discusses the miracles of Jesus.

SCRIPTURE READING

Matthew 8–9, 14–15; Mark 5–7; Luke 8–9; John 5–11

LEARNING OBJECTIVES

1. To discuss the relationship between miracles and divine revelation.

2. To identify the role of miracles in the life of Jesus.

3. To explain the use of the word "miracle" in the New Testament.

QUOTATIONS

It is my observation that Jesus is the ultimate embarrassment to philosophy. Acknowledged to be no less than a great teacher, religious genius, and man of fearless compassion, his life is co-mingled with such astounding events that it has become fashionable to try to keep Jesus human by editing out all taint of the miraculous from the records. This attempt to distinguish the Jesus of history from the divine Christ of faith has not succeeded and seems to involve an intellectual dishonesty that does not hesitate to rewrite the data to support a preconceived theory. For the question 'who was Jesus?' can hardly be answered by assuming at the outset that he was no more than a gifted rabbi, thereby justifying or ignoring or reinterpreting anything that smacks of the supernatural.

—James Gustafson

LECTURE OUTLINE

A. Rudolf Bultmann believed the gospel accounts of Jesus' miracles were mythological stories.
   - The New Testament is often rejected as authoritative and inspired because of its numerous accounts of miracles.

B. A multitude of miracles tend to accompany a new and significant revelation of God in the Scriptures.
   1. Numerous miracles accompanied the life of Moses in order to assist him in his monumental calling.

   2. Several miracles accompanied the lives and ministries of Elijah and Elisha.

   3. The greatest cluster of miracles occurs with the advent of Christ.

C. Nineteenth-century naturalism denied the existence of miracles and twentieth-century neo-liberalism rejected their historical reality.
   1. Form Criticism examines the Scriptural text and seeks to identify the literary forms in which the text appears.

   2. Miracle stories demonstrate a unique plot pattern of affliction, healing, and resulting amazement.

   3. The first century believers were not primitive and gullible people, but were rather struck with amazement at the deeds of Christ.

   4. Christ's enemies during His ministry claimed Christ performed His miracles by the power of Satan.

D. Nicodemus understood that Jesus would not have been able to do what He did if He was not from God.
   1. The extraordinary nature of miracles would be lost if they were a common occurrence.

2. Everything that occurs in this world is by the power of God, but there is a difference between the ordinary and the extraordinary operation of the power of God.

E. Jesus appealed to His miracles as credentials of His Messiahship.

F. "Therefore we must pay much closer attention to what we have heard, lest we drift away from it. For since the message declared by angels proved to be reliable and every transgression or disobedience received a just retribution, how shall we escape if we neglect such a great salvation? It was declared at first by the Lord, and it was attested to us by those who heard, while God also bore witness by signs and wonders and various miracles and by gifts of the Holy Spirit distributed according to his will" (Heb. 2:1–4).
   1. God bore witness to the identity of Jesus through miracles.

   2. "The primary function of the miracle in the Bible is to be the credit of the Proposer" (John Locke).

   3. Miracles prove the truthfulness of the one who is performing them and prove that He is endorsed and blessed by God.

G. The word "miracle" does not occur in the New Testament, but rather the three words: "signs", "powers", and "wonders".
   1. *Wonders* are works that arouse a sense of awe.

   2. *Powers* are extraordinary superhuman abilities.

   3. *Signs* are events that manifest the activity of God.

H. The resurrection of Christ was the greatest sign proving the identity of Jesus.

BIBLE STUDY

1. Read Luke 8:22–25, the account of Jesus miraculously calming the storm. What does this episode reveal about Him? How might this have challenged what the disciples thought they knew about God's Messiah?

2. Read Matthew 12:38-40; 16:1-4; and Luke 11:16, 29. What are the people really asking for in these verses and why? Had they not been given what they asked for already? What do these verses reveal about these people?

3. After reading Luke 2:34 and 11:30, how can Jesus Himself be considered a "sign"? What did His presence signify?

4. What was a major purpose of Jesus' miracles (see John 2:11; 3:2; 10:25, 38; 14:11; and Acts 2:22)?

5. Building off of the previous purpose, what was the intended result upon the witnesses of His miracles (see Matt. 11:20–24; Luke 10:12–15; John 20:30–31)?

6. Read John 7:2–5. What purpose did Jesus not factor in when performing miracles?

DISCUSSION

1. Why is it important to see that Rudolf Bultmann's ideas on the subject of miracles are wrong? What is at stake?

2. Why is the resurrection of Jesus so central to His role as Messiah?

3. Considering all of what Scripture says about Jesus' miracles, what was the purpose and function of the miracles performed by the apostles?

FOR FURTHER STUDY

Keener, Craig. *A Commentary on the Gospel of Matthew*
France, R.T. *The Gospel of Mark*
Sproul, R.C. *A Walk with God: An Exposition of Luke*
Sproul, R.C. *John* (St. Andrew's Expositional Commentary)
Stein, Robert H. *Luke*
Morris, Leon. *The Gospel According to John*

40

The Caesarea-Philippi Confession

MESSAGE INTRODUCTION

Jesus Christ is the central figure in the New Testament and in all of the Scriptures. He is the son of man, the son of God, and the long awaited Messiah. Yet Jesus maintained a certain subtlety regarding His identity while on earth and distanced Himself from the common messianic expectations of the time as a political and military figure who would bring deliverance from Rome. It was rather only to those closest to Him that He revealed His true identity and mission. In this lecture, Dr. Sproul discusses the Caesarea-Philippi confession.

SCRIPTURE READING

Matthew 16; Mark 8; Luke 9:18–27

LEARNING OBJECTIVES

1. To define the Messianic Secret.

2. To define the names of Jesus and Christ.

3. To identify and define the titles of Jesus given in the Gospels.

QUOTATIONS

Jesus did not ask this question to seek information. He was perfectly aware of what other men were calling Him. What He wanted was to prepare the Twelve for the question of all questions. What was their conception of Him? Had He succeeded in imparting to them any understanding as to His identity and mission? They had observed Him for possibly three years. But had they discerned Him? That there was something unusual about Jesus was evident in their replies to His first question. But that was not enough. If the Twelve shared only these popular ideas about Him, then He had failed. But the time had arrived when He needed to know. And so, perhaps with baited breath, Jesus put to them the supreme question. "But whom say ye that I am?"

—Herschel H. Hobbs

LECTURE OUTLINE

A. Jesus Christ is the central figure in the New Testament and in all of the Scriptures.
    1. *Jesus* is the Greek translation of the Hebrew name *Joshua*, which means "the Lord saves".

    2. *Christ* is the Greek translation of the Hebrew title *Messiah.*

B. The "Messianic Secret" is Jesus' subtlety regarding His messianic identity.
    •   Jesus most frequently referred to Himself as the "Son of Man."

C. The messianic expectations of the first-century Jews were of a military conquer or or political leader who would drive the Roman forces from Palestine.
    1. Many Jews of Jesus' day sought to establish an independent nation with the Messiah as their king.

    2. Jesus was reluctant to identify Himself with the messianic title because of all the immediate political expectations placed upon it.

D. "Now when Jesus came into the district of Caesarea Philippi, he asked his disciples, 'Who do people say that the Son of Man is?'" (Matt. 16:13).
    •   Jesus directs this important question to His disciples.

E. "And they said, 'Some say John the Baptist, others say Elijah and others Jeremiah or one of the prophets'" (Matt. 16:14).
    1. Jesus' ministry seemed to resemble John the Baptist's message so some people believed John had risen from the dead.

    2. Jesus was also identified as Elijah due to Malachi's prophecy of the return of Elijah (Malachi 4:5–6).

    3. The most popular opinion was that Jesus was a great prophet.

F. "He said to them, 'But who do you say that I am?'" (Matt. 16:15).
- Jesus now directs this very important question directly to His disciples.

G. "Simon Peter replied, 'You are the Christ, the Son of the living God'" (Matt. 16:16).
- Peter identifies Jesus as the Messiah, the Son of God.

H. The three titles of "son of man", "Christ", and "son of God" are all ascribed to Jesus in this passage.
1. The title "son of God" is granted to those who demonstrate obedience to the Father for sonship is identified by submission.

2. Jesus identified the Pharisees as sons of the devil because they obeyed the Evil One rather than the Father.

3. The title "son of man" is an allusion to the heavenly vision recorded in Daniel 7 in which one like the son of man comes to judge the earth.

4. By referring to Himself as the son of man Jesus could maintain the secret of His messianic office and claim divine authority.

I. "And Jesus answered him, 'Blessed are you, Simon Bar-Jonah! For flesh and blood has not revealed this to you, but my Father who is in heaven'" (Matt. 16:17).
- The Holy Spirit illumined the mind of Simon so that he could identify Jesus as the Messiah.

J. "And I tell you, you are Peter, and on this rock I will build my church, and the gates of hell shall not prevail against it. I will give you the keys of the kingdom of heaven, and whatever you bind on earth shall be bound in heaven, and whatever you loose on earth shall be loosed in heaven" (Matt. 16:18–19).
1. The Roman Catholic church bases its belief in the papacy on this passage.

2. Protestant churches usually interpret this passage to mean that the church will be built upon Peter's confession that Jesus is the Christ.

K. "Then he strictly charged the disciples to tell no one that he was the Christ" (Matt. 16:20).
1. The fundamental mission of the church is to declare that Jesus is the Christ.

2. Jesus encouraged others to keep His messianic mission a secret during His ministry.

L. "From that time Jesus began to show his disciples that he must go to Jerusalem and suffer many things from the elders and chief priests and scribes, and be killed, and on the third day be raised. And Peter took him aside and began to rebuke him, saying, 'Far be it from you, Lord! This shall never happen to you'" (Matt. 16:21–22).
   • Peter cannot see Jesus as the Messiah and as the suffering servant.

M. "But he turned and said to Peter, 'Get behind me, Satan! You are a hindrance to me. For you are not setting your mind on the things of God, but on the things of man'" (Matt. 16:23).
   • Jesus recognizes Peter's words as another attempt by Satan to deter Jesus away from the cross.

BIBLE STUDY

1. Read Matthew 16. This passage begins and ends with references to the fact that no one but the disciples knew Jesus' true identity. The middle portion contains Peter's confession that Jesus is the Christ, which prompts Jesus' promise of the keys of the kingdom of heaven. What does this passage teach about the kingdom?

2. According to Matthew 16 and other passages, what misconceptions of Jesus' identity were circulating at this point in Jesus' ministry? How does Peter come to an accurate conception of Jesus as the Christ?

3. It has been suggested that the "rock" (v. 18) on which Jesus will build His church is Peter, Jesus, Peter's confession, or Peter as a type for all believers. Which view(s) do(es) the text most clearly support?

4. What is the relationship between Jesus building His church on "this rock" and His giving the keys to "you" (in Greek, the "you" is singular)? Why would this have been important to the early church (for whom the Gospels were initially written)?

5. What is the significance of the titles that Peter ascribes to Christ in Matthew 16:16? How does Jesus fulfill the requirements of each of these roles?

6. What is the Old Testament background for the title "son of man" (see Dan. 7:13–14)? Why did Jesus use this title most often to refer to Himself?

DISCUSSION

1. Why does Jesus warn His disciples about the teachings of the Pharisees and Sadducees in Matthew 16:5–12? What were the primary characteristics of their teachings? How are these ideas present among us today?

2. In what sense does the church prevail against the gates of hell (Matt. 16:18)? What kind of authority does the church have on earth to bind and to loose (v. 19)?

3. In Matthew 16:21–23, Peter goes almost immediately from true confession to rebellion and deceit. What does this say about the nature of man—whether or not we've had the truth of God's gospel revealed to us?

FOR FURTHER STUDY

Keener, Craig. *A Commentary on the Gospel of Matthew*
France, R.T. *The Gospel of Mark*
Sproul, R.C. *A Walk with God: An Exposition of Luke*
Stein, Robert H. *Luke*

41

The Transfiguration

MESSAGE INTRODUCTION

The glory of God is a theme of supreme importance in the Scriptures. When Jesus was incarnated as a man He set aside the glory He had always enjoyed at the throne of His Father and humbled Himself. He humbled Himself to take on the flesh of a man and humbled Himself even further to suffer and die as an innocent sacrifice for sinners. He was then exalted in His resurrection and ascension and today sits beside His Father interceding for His people. Yet the glory Jesus exudes currently was exhibited briefly to Peter, James, and John one day during Christ's earthly ministry. He gave these three a vision of the coming glory of the kingdom that they never forgot. In this lecture, Dr. Sproul discusses the transfiguration.

SCRIPTURE READING

Matthew 17–20; Mark 9–10; Luke 9:28–36

LEARNING OBJECTIVES

1. To identify the meaning of the word *glory* in the Scriptures.

2. To understand the trend of humiliation and exaltation in the life of Christ.

3. To assess the significance of the transfiguration of Jesus.

QUOTATIONS

[This] event gives insight to these privileged disciples about where God's plan is headed. Jesus is not just a meek Galilean teacher, nor should he be seen as someone who merely calls on us to love one another, perhaps the most popular current image of Jesus.

He is not the equal of Moses, Mohammed, or Joseph Smith. These current popular perceptions of Jesus are a major distortion of who he is. He is the glorified and chosen one of God, who one day will manifest himself with all the glory that the mountain scene revealed.

—Darrell L. Bock

LECTURE OUTLINE

A. The Hebrew word for glory is *kabod*.
1. The root of the word *kabod* implies "heaviness" or "weightiness."

2. The word conveys the idea of supreme importance or dignity in the Hebrew Scriptures.

B. The Scriptures speak frequently regarding the glory of God.

C. Jesus set aside His glory to be incarnated as a man and to enter His humiliation.
1. The progress of Jesus' ministry moves from humiliation to exaltation.

2. The birth, rejection, and passion of Jesus were all parts of Jesus' humiliation.

3. The resurrection and ascension were parts of Jesus' exaltation.

D. Despite a general trend from humiliation to exaltation in the life of Jesus there are moments when the glory of God is truly displayed in the life of Christ.

E. "And after six days Jesus took with him Peter and James, and John his brother, and led them up a high mountain by themselves. And he was transfigured before them" (Matt. 17:1–2a).
1. A *transfiguration* is a metamorphosis or transformation.

2. Jesus' transfiguration is a temporary display of the glory of God.

F. "And he was transfigured before them, and his face shone like the sun, and his clothes became white as light" (Matt. 17:2).
1. Saul was blinded by the glory of God that is described as brighter than the noonday sun (Acts 9).

2. The human eye winces to look into the brightness of the sun.

3. Mark declares that Jesus' garments became whiter than any fuller or launderer could make them (Mark 9:3).

4. Jesus' glory was not simply a reflected glory.

5. Moses was privileged to see the back of God's glory in Exodus 33 and the Israelites could not bear to look at his unveiled face afterwards.

6. Amidst the disciples' fears regarding the days to come, God gives them a vision of the glory of His Son.

G. "And behold, there appeared to them Moses and Elijah, talking with him. And Peter said to Jesus, 'Lord, it is good that we are here. If you wish, I will make three tents here, one for you and one for Moses and one for Elijah.' He was still speaking when, behold, a bright cloud overshadowed them, and a voice from the cloud said, 'This is my beloved Son, with whom I am well pleased; listen to him.' When the disciples heard this, they fell on their faces and were terrified" (Matt. 17:1–6).

1. Moses represents the law and Elijah represents the prophets for both of these spoke of the coming of Christ.

2. A voice from above tells the disciples to listen to Jesus.

3. Jesus touches them and tells them to stand up.

4. This is a turning point for the disciples and they proceed with Jesus on to Jerusalem.

BIBLE STUDY

1. Read Exodus 33:17–34:9. Why does Moses' face shine? How does this compare to the reason Jesus radiates glory? Why would this be significant for Israelites who were trying to verify Jesus' claims?

2. Look back at Matthew 17:1–8. Peter's reverence for Moses as the mediator of the law and for Elijah as a preeminent prophet is evident in his desire to build them tabernacles. How could Peter have known that this desire was inappropriate? What does this reveal about Peter's understanding of Jesus' identity? What does the Father's response reveal about Jesus' identity itself?

3. Closely examine Matthew 16:24–28, the prelude to the transfiguration. Is Jesus' coming in His kingdom the same as His coming in the glory of His Father? Why or why not? Do you think that Jesus has already ascended to the throne as king of the universe?

4. Shortly after the transfiguration, the account of Jesus and the temple tax is recorded (Matt. 17:24–27). How does Jesus identify Himself as the royal son of a greater kingdom while at the same time submitting to earthly authorities? What does this suggest to Christ's followers in every age, who live as sojourners in the midst of the tension between this world and the world to come?

5. Matthew 19:13–15 records the famous event of the little children being received by Jesus. What does this passage plainly teach? What is it about children that Jesus wished to commend to those present?

DISCUSSION

1. Compare Moses' and the disciples' reactions to seeing God's glory. How are they alike? How are they different? How does God respond to them in light of their reactions?

2. How do your views on whether or not Jesus has already ascended the throne of heaven, that God's kingdom is already underway, affect the way you live, the way you perceive blessing and suffering, and the nature of spiritual warfare?

3. In light of Matthew 20:20–28, what is to characterize leaders in Christ's kingdom? How does Jesus provide the perfect model of this through His life (and death; see Isa. 50:4–11; 53:10–11)?

FOR FURTHER STUDY

Keener, Craig. *A Commentary on the Gospel of Matthew*
France, R.T. *The Gospel of Mark*
Sproul, R.C. *A Walk with God: An Exposition of Luke*
Stein, Robert H. *Luke*

42

The Triumphal Entry

MESSAGE INTRODUCTION

The triumphal entry was one of the greatest moments in the life of Jesus. Riding into Jerusalem on a donkey amidst shouts of "Hosannas!" and royal proclamations, it seemed like Jesus was going to finally fulfill the role of the Messiah and overthrow the enemies of the people. At last Jesus would use His powers against the Roman oppressors. Yet if these were the expectations of the crowd they were bitterly disappointed a few days later. For Jesus had indeed come to defeat the enemies of His people, but He would do so through suffering rather than the sword. Misunderstanding Jesus' mission, the crowd's shout of "Hosanna!" would change to "Crucify him!" a few days later. In this lecture, Dr. Sproul discusses the triumphal entry.

SCRIPTURE READING

Matthew 21–25; Mark 11–13; Luke 19; John 12–17

LEARNING OBJECTIVES

1. To identify the significance of the triumphal entry in the ministry of Jesus.

2. To define the meaning and symbolism of the word *hosanna*.

3. To discuss the relationship between the Apocrypha and the Scriptures.

QUOTATIONS

Formerly, during His public ministry, Jesus had, as a rule, refused to be openly honored as Messiah. Now, however, the moment has arrived when He is going to announce Himself as the promised King in the centre of the Holy Land so that the people can finally take sides for or against Him. Nevertheless He is not going to appear with outward power, but will enter the holy city as Prince of Peace.

—Norval Geldenhuys

LECTURE OUTLINE

A. The New Testament assigns great significance to the triumphal entry of Jesus into Jerusalem.

B. "And when he had said these things, he went on ahead, going up to Jerusalem. When he drew near to Bethphage and Bethany, at the mount that is called Olivet, he sent two of the disciples, saying, 'Go into the village in front of you, where on entering you will find a colt tied, on which no one has ever yet sat. Untie it and bring it here. If anyone asks you, "Why are you untying it?" you shall say this: "The Lord has need of it"'" (Luke 19:28–31).

C. The triumphal entry was one of the first occasions in which Jesus identifies Himself with Old Testament prophecies regarding the Messiah.

D. "This took place to fulfill what was spoken by the prophet, saying, 'Say to the daughter of Zion, "Behold, your king is coming to you, humble, and mounted on a donkey, and on a colt, the foal of a beast of burden."'" The disciples went and did as Jesus had directed them. They brought the donkey and the colt and put on them their cloaks, and he sat on them. Most of the crowd spread their cloaks on the road, and others cut branches from the trees and spread them on the road. And the crowds that went before him and that followed him were shouting, 'Hosanna to the Son of David! Blessed is he who comes in the name of the Lord! Hosanna in the highest!'" (Matt. 21:6–9).
   1. A dignitary is given honor when we roll out a red carpet for him.

   2. Jesus was honored by people placing their garments on the donkey so that He could ride comfortably.

   3. Garments and palm branches were laid down before the donkey's path as a gesture of honor to Jesus.

E. The crowds shouted "Hosanna!" as Jesus entered the city.
   1. The term can indicate exaltation or adoration.

   2. Palm branches were also traditionally known as "hosannas" and used to celebrate a great victory.

   3. The people were celebrating Jesus as the king who would bring them victory over their enemies.

4. The crowd's shout of "hosanna" would be replaced with "crucify him" a couple days later.

5. The people's expectations of a military victory over the Romans were not met and they turned their anger against Jesus.

F. "As he was drawing near—already on the way down the Mount of Olives—the whole multitude of his disciples began to rejoice and praise God with a loud voice for all the mighty works that they had seen, saying, 'Blessed is the King who comes in the name of the Lord! Peace in heaven and glory in the highest!' And some of the Pharisees in the crowd said to him, 'Teacher, rebuke your disciples'" (Luke 19:37–39).
    •   Jesus was a threat to the religious establishment and the religious leaders feared His popularity with the crowd.

G. "He answered, 'I tell you, if these were silent, the very stones would cry out'" (Luke 19:40).
    •   Jesus' kingship has cosmic significance whose rule extends over the entire earth.

H. The procession of the triumphal entry begins by going down the Mount of Olives, around the Kidron Valley, and into the gates of Jerusalem.
    •   The people believe Jesus has come to conquer for His kingdom.

I. The Apocrypha is a collection of books written during the Intertestamental Period that are not canonical or inspired books, but do have important historical value in helping us understand the New Testament.
    1. "I, Esdras, saw upon Mount Zion a great people whom I could not number and they all praised the Lord with songs. And in the middle of them there was a young man, higher in stature than them all. And upon every one of their heads he set crowns. He was higher than the others which I much marveled at. So I asked the angel and said, 'who are these my Lord?' who answered and said to me, 'these be they that have put off the mortal clothing and have put on the immortal and have confessed the name of God and now are they crowned and receive the palms.' And then I said unto the angel, 'what young man is it that sets crowns upon them, and gives them palms in their hands?' And he answered and said to me, 'It is the Son of God whom they have confessed in the world.' And then began I greatly to commend them that they had lived so strongly for the name of the Lord" (II Esdras 2:42–47).

    2. The people do not wave the palms here, but rather receive them in their hands from the Son of God.

3. The martyrs receive the symbol of victory in their hands and a crown upon their heads.

4. The Scriptures confirm that those who participate with Christ in His humiliation will also participate with Christ in His exaltation.

5. The King who enters Jerusalem in triumph promises to share the inheritance of His kingdom with all of those who confess His name.

BIBLE STUDY

1. What was the battle context in which Zechariah 9:9 was written? In what sense was the triumphal entry into Jerusalem an act of war?

2. What actions and words of the crowd indicate the people's expectations of Jesus in His role as the Christ? What actions and words of Jesus in Matthew 20:17–21:17 indicate Jesus' own conception of Himself and His role? How do these ideas about His mission clash (or not)?

3. The crowd who welcomed Jesus did so by quoting from Psalm 118:26 and relating the words to Jesus. What in Psalm 118 should have indicated to the crowd that Jesus was going to be exactly the kind of Christ He turned out to be: a rejected, crucified Savior?

4. How does 2 Esdras 2:42–47 (quoted in the outline), while not inspired, nonetheless help us in understanding this event (the triumphal entry)?

5. How did Jesus' cleansing the temple challenge the very ideals of those who welcomed Him and thought He was going to defend Israel (Matt. 21:12–17)? Why was Jesus angered at what was occurring on the temple grounds?

DISCUSSION

1. According to the text, the people believed Jesus to be a prophet, but the chief priests and scribes wanted to kill Him (Matt. 21:11, 46). How did Jesus' presence challenge the chief priests and Pharisees? How did Jesus' kingship threaten their way of life? How does His kingship threaten your way of life?

2. Matthew frequently calls attention to the fact that Jesus' life fulfills scriptural prophecies regarding the Messiah. Remembering that the early church was in the midst of suffering, how do you think they gained confidence in Christ through this knowledge? Does this knowledge give you confidence that Jesus is the Christ?

3. Read Matthew 23:25–26. How are Christians often guilty, like the Pharisees of washing, the outside of the cup while leaving the inside of the cup full of self-preservation and self-indulgence? In what ways do you strive to look good on the outside while secretly hiding selfish motives?

FOR FURTHER STUDY

Keener, Craig. *A Commentary on the Gospel of Matthew*
France, R.T. *The Gospel of Mark*
Sproul, R.C. *A Walk with God: An Exposition of Luke*
Sproul, R.C. *John* (St. Andrew's Expositional Commentary)
Stein, Robert H. *Luke*
Morris, Leon. *The Gospel According to John*

43

The Cross

MESSAGE INTRODUCTION

The Romans made thousands of people victims of crucifixion. Such a brutal and horrific manner of death sent a strong message to those who would consider defying the power of Rome. This imperial muscle flexing was done with efficiency and indifference to the plight of its victim. Jesus of Nazareth was just another victim for the soldiers. None of them realized that the very man they were cursing by nailing Him to a tree was taking the curse of sin upon Himself. The death of Jesus is central in the history of redemption. In this lecture, Dr. Sproul discusses the crucifixion of Christ.

SCRIPTURE READING

Matthew 26–27; Mark 14–15; Luke 22–23; John 18–19

LEARNING OBJECTIVES

1. To identify various perspectives on the crucifixion of Christ.

2. To discuss the forsakenness of Christ on the cross.

3. To describe the role of God the Father in the crucifixion of Christ.

QUOTATIONS

Death by crucifixion was one of the cruelest and most degrading forms of punishment ever conceived by human perversity, even in the eyes of the pagan world. Josephus described it as "the most wretched of all ways of dying," and the shudder caused by the cross as an instrument of execution is still reflected in the English word "excruciating." Yet in the Roman provinces crucifixion was one of the customary means of preserving public order, and the history of turbulent Judea is punctuated by accounts of men being crucified. So unimportant was the crucifixion of Jesus of Nazareth—from a Roman point of view that Tacitus—in his review of the troubles in Judea, comments, "Under Tiberius nothing happened."

In Christian perspective the cross of Christ is the focal point of the gospel. Here God dealt definitively with the problem of human rebellion and made provision for the salvation of men . . . The account of Jesus' crucifixion thus became the center point of the joyful tidings proclaimed by the church, in the conviction that the message centering in the cross was empowered by God to overturn the note of offense and the objections of human cleverness and to bring men into the experience of redemption.

—William L. Lane

LECTURE OUTLINE

A. Crucifixion was the normal method of executing criminals in the Roman Empire.
    1. Thousands of people were executed through crucifixion, but only one victim of crucifixion has their death celebrated internationally each year.

    2. Jesus' crucifixion is significant because it was the death of a king and His death provided an atonement for sin.

B. Pilate viewed Jesus' death as the elimination of a revolutionary.
    1. The religious leaders viewed Jesus' death as expedient to reinforce their religious authority.

    2. The Roman soldiers viewed the crucifixion of Christ as just another death, although the commander confessed his belief in the Son of God.

    3. Few witnesses realized that Jesus was satisfying the demands of God's justice against sinners on the cross.

C. "And over his head they put the charge against him, which read, 'This is Jesus, the King of the Jews.' Then two robbers were crucified with him, one on the right and one on the left. And those who passed by derided him, wagging their heads and saying, 'you who would destroy the temple and rebuild it in three days, save yourself! If you are the Son of God, come down from the cross.' So also the chief priests, with the scribes and elders, mocked him, saying, 'He saved others; he cannot save himself. He is the King of Israel let him come down now from the cross, and we will believe in him. He trusts in God; let God deliver him now, if he desires him. For he said, "I am the Son of God."' And the robbers who were crucified with him also reviled him in the same way" (Matt. 27:37–44).
    • The gospel writers label the mocking of the crowd as blasphemy because Jesus was deity.

D. "Now from the sixth hour there was darkness over all the land until the ninth hour. And about the ninth hour Jesus cried out with a loud voice, saying, 'Eli, Eli, lema sabachthani?' that is, 'My God, my God, why have you forsaken me?'" (Matt. 27:45–46).

   1. Why would Jesus who was the perfect Son of God cry out from the cross that God had forsaken Him?

   2. Jesus is quoting Psalm 22 with these words.

E. Jesus did not simply *feel* forsaken, but rather He truly *was* forsaken by God.

   1. Jesus had to bear in Himself the full measure of divine punishment in order to satisfy the demands of God's justice.

   2. Jesus became the most obscene thing in all of creation on the cross because concentrated on Him was the corporate wickedness of every man.

   3. The punishment of hell and the full measure of divine forsakenness was placed upon Jesus.

F. "O foolish Galatians! Who has bewitched you? It was before your eyes that Jesus Christ was publicly portrayed as crucified" (Gal. 3:1).

   1. Paul proceeds to discuss the relevance of the crucifixion for the Galatian believers.

   2. "So then, those who are of faith are blessed along with Abraham, the man of faith. For all who rely on works of the law are under a curse; for it is written, 'Cursed be everyone who does not abide by all things written in the Book of the Law, and do them.' Now it is evident that no one is justified before God by the law, for 'The righteous shall live by faith.' But the law is not of faith, rather 'The one who does them shall live by them.' Christ redeemed us from the curse of the law by becoming a curse for us—for it is written, 'Cursed is everyone who is hanged on a tree'" (Gal. 3:9–13).

G. Paul elaborates on the significance of Christ's death by referring to Jewish law rather than Roman law.

   1. God outlined a series of blessings for obedience and curses for disobedience.

   2. The disobedient were hung on a tree as a curse; and Christ took this curse upon Himself.

H. The Day of Atonement featured two significant symbolic acts.

   1. A lamb was slaughtered to make atonement for sins.

2. The sin of the covenant community was transferred to the scapegoat which was released outside the camp.

I. Paul looks at the cross of Christ as satisfying the curse of the law because Jesus becomes the curse.
    1. The symbolic acts of the Day of Atonement foreshadowed the work of Christ.

    2. Jesus was not stoned in accordance with Jewish law because such a death would not fulfill the law of God.

J. Jesus was handed over to the Gentiles in accordance with the prophets' words.

K. Jesus was crucified at Golgotha outside the walls of Jerusalem just as the scapegoat bearing the sins of the people was sent outside the camp.

L. Darkness descends on the land as Jesus expires on the cross.

M. The priests blessed the people of Israel with the following blessing.
    1. "The LORD bless you and keep you; the LORD make his face to shine upon you and be gracious to you; the LORD lift up his countenance upon you and give you peace" (Num. 6:24–26).

    2. The supreme blessing for the Israelites was the favorable gaze of God.

    3. The ultimate promise for the Israelite was the hope of one day seeing God's face in all His glory.

N. God the Father turns the lights out and turns His back on His Son as He has become the incarnation of human sin.
    • Jesus cries out regarding the forsakenness He feels as He experiences the full agony of God's abandonment and hell.

O. Jesus declares, "It is finished" and, "Into thy hands I commit my spirit," as His last words.
    • In the midst of His abandonment Jesus trusts His Father and drinks the cup of divine wrath for us.

BIBLE STUDY

1. What use did the blood of lambs and goats have under the old covenant? Consider the following verses in your answer: Ex. 24:8; Lev. 8:22–24; 14:14, 25; Zech. 9:11. What use does blood have in the new covenant (see Jer. 31:31; Matt. 26:27–29)?

2. Read Exodus 16; John 6:35; and Hebrews 9:13–15. What is the significance of the particular elements Jesus chooses to use during the Last Supper?

3. Much of John 19:1–16 is portrayed in what is called "dramatic irony." Something is considered "ironic" if there is something the writer and reader know about a character that makes the events recorded more significant. Since you, the reader, understand John's previous portrayal of Jesus as the eternal God who has become flesh, ask yourself what is ironic about:

   a) the way Jesus is dressed in verses 1–3?
   b) the charge made against Him in verse 7?
   c) Pilate's question in verse 9?
   d) Pilate's claim to power in verse 10?
   e) who is sitting on the judgment seat in verse 13?

4. How is Jesus' greatest moment of humiliation also a great moment of triumph? How does the cross fulfill the promise found in Genesis 3:15?

5. What do the dramatic events that occur in connection with the death of Jesus recorded in Matthew 27:50–53 symbolize?

6. What did Jesus mean with His words "It is finished"? What was "finished" at that time? What, consequently, was begun?

DISCUSSION

1. Looking over John 19 and remembering that the author's reason for writing his gospel is so that "you may believe that Jesus is the Christ, the Son of God, and that believing you may have life in His name," how does this chapter accomplish this goal?

2. Why does the announcement of betrayal shock Jesus' disciples? How was Judas able to blend in with the other eleven over the course of His ministry?

3. In the Garden of Gethsemane Jesus prays, "Father, if you are willing, remove this cup from me. Nevertheless, not my will, but yours be done" (Luke 22:42). Consider an area of your life—both corporately as a church and individually as one member of the body—in which this prayer could or should apply.

FOR FURTHER STUDY

Keener, Craig. *A Commentary on the Gospel of Matthew*
France, R.T. *The Gospel of Mark*
Sproul, R.C. *John* (St. Andrew's Expositional Commentary)
Sproul, R.C. *The Truth of the Cross*
Stein, Robert H. *Luke*

44

The Resurrection

MESSAGE INTRODUCTION

The horror of the crucifixion crushed any lingering hopes among the disciples that Jesus was the long awaited Messiah. Their despair was so powerful that they refused to believe the reports that Jesus had indeed risen from the grave. The reports of the women and the open tomb were suggestive, but it was too painful for them to get their hopes up again. Only the physical appearance of Jesus Himself and His rebuke about their refusal to believe finally convinced them that Jesus had indeed conquered the grave. The resurrection revived their faith in Him as their Messiah and gave them hope that they too would conquer the grave through Him. In this lecture, Dr. Sproul discusses the resurrection.

SCRIPTURE READING

Matthew 28; Mark 16; Luke 24; John 20–21

LEARNING OBJECTIVES

1. To describe the significance of the Valley of Gehenna in Jewish thought.

2. To describe the reaction of the disciples to the resurrection of Jesus.

3. To discuss the appearance of Jesus on the road to Emmaus.

QUOTATIONS

Our Lord . . . deliberately staked his whole claim upon his resurrection. When asked for a sign, he repeatedly pointed to this sign as his single and sufficient credential

(John 2:19; Matt. 12:40). The earliest proclaimers of the gospel conceived witnessing to the resurrection of their Master as their primary function (Acts 1:22; 2: 32; 4:33; 10:41; 17:18). The lively hope and steadfast faith that sprang up within them they ascribed to its power (1 Peter 1:3; 1:21; 3:21). Paul's whole gospel was the gospel of the risen Savior.

—B.B. Warfield

LECTURE OUTLINE

A. The resurrection is part of the exaltation of Christ, but probably not the beginning.
    •   The nadir of Christ's humiliation is His death on the cross.

B. The bodies of most victims of crucifixion were tossed into the burning garbage heap outside the city.
    1. The Valley of Gehenna became associated in the Jewish mind with hell.

    2. Garbage was dumped at Gehenna every day and therefore it became a place where the worms did not die and the fires would not go out.

C. The body of Jesus was not brought to Gehenna, but placed in the tomb of a rich man secured by Joseph of Arimathea.
    •   Isaiah prophesied regarding Jesus' burial saying "and they made his grave with the wicked and with a rich man in his death" (Isa. 53:9a).

D. The resurrection is a central feature of the exaltation of Christ.

E. "But on the first day of the week, at early dawn, they went to the tomb, taking the spices they had prepared. And they found the stone rolled away from the tomb, but when they went in they did not find the body of the Lord Jesus" (Luke 24:1–3).
    1. The belief in the resurrection does not rest simply on the idea that there was an empty tomb.

    2. The belief in the resurrection is based on eyewitness accounts recorded in the New Testament.

F. "While they were perplexed about this, behold, two men stood by them in dazzling apparel. And as they were frightened and bowed their faces to the ground, the men said to them, 'Why do you seek the living among the dead? He is not here, but has risen'" (Luke 24:6a).
    •   The announcement of Jesus' resurrection is one of the most dramatic in all of Scripture.

G. "Remember how he told you, while he was still in Galilee, that the Son of Man must be delivered into the hands of sinful men and be crucified and on the third day rise.' And they remembered his words, and returning from the tomb they told all these things to the eleven and to all the rest. Now it was Mary Magdalene and Joanna, and Mary the mother of James, and the other women with them, who told these things to the apostles, but these words seemed to them an idle tale, and they did not believe them" (Luke 24:6b–11).

1. People living in first-century Palestine were not naïve and superstitious simpletons.

2. The disciples initially rejected the resurrection report of the women who went to the tomb.

H. "But Peter rose and ran to the tomb; stooping and looking in, he saw the linen cloths by themselves; and he went home marveling at what had happened" (Luke 24:12).

• The disciples are nevertheless curious enough to investigate the reports of the women.

I. "That very day two of them were going to a village named Emmaus, about seven miles from Jerusalem, and they were talking with each other about all these things that had happened. While they were talking and discussing together, Jesus himself drew near and went with them. But their eyes were kept from recognizing him" (Luke 24:13–16).

1. Jesus was not unrecognizable to these two disciples, but rather the Spirit of God withheld them from identifying Jesus.

2. The hopes of the disciples were completely dashed on the day of the crucifixion.

3. The grief of the disciples hindered their ability to recognize Jesus after His resurrection.

J. "And he said to them, 'What is this conversation that you are holding with each other as you walk?' And they stood still, looking sad. Then one of them, named Cleopas, answered him, 'Are you the only visitor to Jerusalem who does not know the things that have happened there in these days?'" (Luke 24:17–18).

• Cleopas is shocked at his fellow traveler's apparent ignorance of recent events in Jerusalem.

K. "And he said to them, 'What things?' And they said to him, 'Concerning Jesus of Nazareth, a man who was a prophet mighty in deed and word before God and all the people, and how our chief priests and rulers delivered him up to be condemned to death, and crucified him. But we had hoped that he was the one to redeem Israel'" (Luke 24:19–21a).

- These disciples grieve because their expectations of a Messiah as a military hero have not been met.

L. "Moreover, some women of our company amazed us. They were at the tomb early in the morning, and when they did not find his body, they came back saying that they had even seen a vision of angels, who said that he was alive. Some of those who were with us went to the tomb and found it just as the women had said, but him they did not see" (Luke 24:22–24).

- These disciples do not believe the report of the women because they did not see Jesus Himself.

M. "And he said to them, 'O foolish ones, and slow of heart to believe all that the prophets have spoken! Was it not necessary that the Christ should suffer these things and enter into his glory?' And beginning with Moses and all the Prophets, he interpreted to them in all the Scriptures the things concerning himself" (Luke 24:25–27).

- Jesus shows these two men how all of the law and Prophets spoke about His coming.

N. "So they drew near to the village to which they were going. He acted as if he were going farther, but they urged him strongly, saying, 'Stay with us, for it is toward evening and the day is now far spent.' So he went in to stay with them. When he was at table with them, he took the bread and blessed and broke it and gave it to them. And their eyes were opened, and they recognized him. And he vanished from their sight" (Luke 24:28–31).

- As the disciples shared a meal with Jesus their eyes were briefly opened and they recognized Him before He vanished in front of them.

O. "They said to each other, 'Did not our hearts burn within us while he talked to us on the road, while he opened to us the Scriptures?' And they rose that same hour and returned to Jerusalem. And they found the eleven and those who were with them gathered together, saying, 'The Lord has risen indeed, and has appeared to Simon!' Then they told what had happened on the road, and how he was known to them in the breaking of the bread. As they were talking about these things, Jesus himself stood among them, and said to them, 'Peace to you!'" (Luke 24:32–36).

1. Most moderns consider the resurrection of a dead man to be impossible.

2. Jesus bore the sins of others in His death and not His own.

3. The Scriptures declare that it was impossible for death to hold Jesus.

4. Death could not hold Jesus in the grave, and the Father could not conceal His sinless son in hell without raising Him to life again.

BIBLE STUDY

1. Why is it so important to authentic Christian faith to believe that Jesus rose from the dead? Given that the disciples had been told by Jesus Himself who He was and what would happen to Him, why do you suppose the disciples were so slow to believe He had risen from the dead?

2. Examine the three supernatural appearances detailed in Luke 24:1–49 (the angels at the tomb, Jesus on the road to Emmaus, and Jesus in Jerusalem). What do the messages in each instance have in common? Are there any significant differences?

3. After Jesus' resurrection, the Jews spread a rumor that Jesus' body had been stolen and that the disciples had fabricated the resurrection story (see Matt. 28:11–15). What evidence in this passage refutes this rumor? In Luke's account, how many witnesses attested to the fact that Jesus' body had been stolen? How many witnesses attested to the fact that He had risen from the dead? How reliable were the witnesses?

4. How can Jesus claim all authority and power under heaven and earth after His resurrection (Matt. 28:18)? Why is this truth especially important as the disciples (and, by extension, the church) receive the Great Commission in Matthew 28:18–20?

5. What does it mean that Christ Jesus is "the resurrection and the life" (John 11:25)?

DISCUSSION

1. What is ironic about the despair of the men on the road to Emmaus? How does their despair indicate that they misunderstood much that Jesus had taught them? It what ways does your thinking reflect their own?

2. What are the strongest arguments you know against the bodily resurrection of Jesus? How do you respond?

3. According to Jesus, the Old Testament teaches about Him, even addressing His death and resurrection. As you read the Old Testament, do you look for these elements? What does Luke 24:45 suggest is necessary to properly understand the Scriptures? If you believe this verse, how would it change your approach to Bible Study?

FOR FURTHER STUDY

Keener, Craig. *A Commentary on the Gospel of Matthew*
France, R.T. *The Gospel of Mark*
Stein, Robert H. *Luke*
Morris, Leon. *The Gospel According to John*

45

The Ascension

MESSAGE INTRODUCTION

The hearts of the disciples were filled with sorrow upon Jesus' announcement that He would depart from them. They had walked with their Lord since the beginning of His ministry and the thought of His absence only provoked grief. Yet the ascension of Jesus into heaven was necessary so that He could prepare a place for them and then they could be reunited. The Holy Spirit would dwell within them in the meantime and minister to their hearts as a down payment of their future inheritance. Appreciating these promises and filled with hope regarding the future, the disciples were filled with joy and moved to rejoicing as Jesus ascended to heaven. In this lecture, Dr. Sproul discusses the ascension.

SCRIPTURE READING

Luke 24:50–53; Acts 1

LEARNING OBJECTIVES

1. To identify the grief and fear of Jesus' disciples at the Last Supper.

2. To detail Jesus' promises to His disciples at the Last Supper.

3. To describe the purpose of Jesus' ascension.

QUOTATIONS

The significance of the ascension is often overlooked in the modern church. We have special celebrations and holidays (holy days) to commemorate the birth (Christmas), the death (Good Friday), and the resurrection (Easter) of Christ. Most churches, however, make little or no mention of the ascension. However, the ascension is a redemptive event of profound importance. It marks the moment of Christ's highest point of exaltation prior to His return. It is in the ascension that Christ entered into His glory.

—R.C. Sproul

LECTURE OUTLINE

A. John 14 is one of the most popular chapters in the Bible.
  1. "Let not your hearts be troubled. Believe in God; believe also in me. In my Father's house are many rooms. If it were not so, would I have told you that I go to prepare a place for you? And if I go and prepare a place for you, I will come again and will take you to myself, that where I am you may be also. And you know the way to where I am going" (John 14:1–3).

  2. Jesus originally spoke these words in a context of fear and confusion among the disciples.

B. "When he had gone out, Jesus said, 'Now is the Son of Man glorified, and God is glorified in him. If God is glorified in him, God will also glorify him in himself, and glorify him at once. Little children, yet a little while I am with you. You will seek me, and just as I said to the Jews, so now I also say to you, 'Where I am going you cannot come.' A new commandment I give to you, that you love one another: just as I have loved you, you also are to love one another. By this all people will know that you are my disciples, if you have love for one another'" (John 13:31–35).
  1. Jesus forecasted His departure into death in the upper room, but His disciples failed to understand.

  2. Jesus told them to not let their hearts be troubled because He knew they would be crushed with grief by the humiliation of His death.

  3. Jesus assures His disciples that if they were living with a false hope regarding the resurrection of the dead then He would have told them.

  4. If we truly believed Jesus left us to prepare a place for us, our longing for heaven would increase and our whole view of heaven would change.

C. "I have said these things to you to keep you from falling away. They will put you out of the synagogues. Indeed, the hour is coming when whoever kills you will think he is offering service to God. And they will do these things because they have not known the Father, nor me. But I have said these things to you, that when their hour comes you may remember that I told them to you. I did not say these things to you from the beginning, because I was with you. But now I am going to him who sent me, and none of you asks me, 'Where are you going?' But because I have said these things to you, sorrow has filled your heart" (John 16:1–6).

- The pain of Jesus' departure was the focus of the disciples on the night of the Last Supper.

D. Luke provides two accounts of the ascension. One at the beginning of Acts and the other at the end of his gospel.

1. "And while staying with them he ordered them not to depart from Jerusalem, but to wait for the promise of the Father, which, he said, 'you heard from me; for John baptized with water, but you will be baptized with the Holy Spirit not many days from now.' So when they had come together, they asked him, 'Lord, will you at this time restore the kingdom to Israel?' He said to them, 'It is not for you to know times or seasons that the Father has fixed by his own authority. But you will receive power when the Holy Spirit has come upon you, and you will be my witnesses in Jerusalem and in all Judea and Samaria, and to the end of the earth.' And when he had said these things, as they were looking on, he was lifted up, and a cloud took him out of their sight. And while they were gazing into heaven as he went, behold, two men stood by them in white robes, and said, 'Men of Galilee, why do you stand looking into heaven? This Jesus, who was taken up from you into heaven, will come in the same way as you saw him go into heaven'" (Acts 1:4–11).

2. "Then he led them out as far as Bethany, and lifting up his hands he blessed them. While he blessed them, he parted from them and was carried up into heaven. And they worshiped him and returned to Jerusalem with great joy, and were continually in the temple blessing God" (Luke 24:50–53).

E. The significance of the ascension is often forgotten.

1. The disciples rejoiced greatly and praised God continually upon the ascension of Jesus to heaven.

2. The disciples were able to rejoice because they came to an understanding of why Jesus left and what He would be doing for them.

F. Jesus ascends to His heavenly throne for His coronation.

1. He is invested as the king who conquered death on our behalf.

2. The ascension is a cause for rejoicing for all Christians because our king reigns from now on for us.

3. The task of the church is to make the invisible reign of Jesus Christ visible by our fidelity, celebration, and joy.

4. Jesus will return to consummate the establishment of His heavenly kingdom on earth.

BIBLE STUDY

1. Many people believe the resurrection of Christ is the high point of redemptive history. After studying the event known as the ascension, you might rethink this. Focusing on Acts 1:1–11, who is present in this scene? When did it take place? Where were they? What does it say about the progression of the gospel? How does the book of Acts detail the fulfillment of these words?

2. What did the Father promise in Acts 1:4–5? What power was to be received with the promise? What was the purpose for this power? How was the promise related to Jesus' ascension (compare John 16:5–16)?

3. Examine Jesus' response to the apostle's question about the kingdom of Israel (Acts 1:6). Of which kingdom did the apostles speak? On what did Jesus refocus their attention? Did Jesus say or imply that the kingdom actually would be restored to Israel?

4. Where did Jesus go when He ascended? According to Luke's gospel account (24:50–52) of this event, the disciples rejoiced at His leaving. Why would they do that? Could it be connected to where Jesus was going and why (John 14)?

5. It has always been a point of Christian doctrine that Jesus retained His resurrected human body when He ascended, though many Christians today make the mistake of associating heaven with all things ethereal (and thus that Jesus did not continue on in His physical body). What do the "men in white robes" say happened to Jesus' body? Given the rumors about the whereabouts of Jesus' body, why was this information included?

6. The two men in white (probably angels) seem to reprove the apostles for staring into the sky after Jesus. Explain their statements. If Jesus is coming back in the same way He left, why shouldn't the apostles stare after Him? Why do you think the men emphasized to the apostles that Jesus was coming back?

DISCUSSION

1. How does the formation of the church begin the period of the restoration of the kingdom? Through what means does the kingdom's restoration continue today? What event will complete the kingdom's restoration? Is it possible for the church to usher in the kingdom's full restoration just prior to Christ's return? Why or why not?

2. The ascension is important because it marks the beginning of the spread of the gospel and the promised empowerment of God's people. Do you perceive yourself as a fully empowered Christian? What can you do to stop disbelieving who the Bible says you are in Christ?

3. Why do the disciples feel compelled to choose another disciple to replace Judas (Acts 1:22b)? What is the qualification they seek in the man to replace Judas?

FOR FURTHER STUDY

Dawson, Gerrit Scott. *Jesus Ascended*
Johnson, Dennis E. *The Message of Acts in the History of Redemption*
Kistemaker, Simon. *Exposition of the Acts of the Apostles*

46

Pentecost

MESSAGE INTRODUCTION

The Holy Spirit that Jesus promised to His disciples came upon the early believers on the day of Pentecost. Henceforth the church was empowered and gifted to fulfill God's purposes on the earth. The pouring out of the Spirit on all believers was the fulfillment of a prophecy made by Joel several hundred years before the day of Pentecost. Yet one of the earliest distributions of the Spirit occurred in the wilderness under the leadership of Moses to the other elders of Israel. The Spirit that came upon Old Testament believers on limited occasions for specific ministries was finally given to all of God's people on the day of Pentecost. In this lecture, Dr. Sproul discusses the day of Pentecost.

SCRIPTURE READING

Acts 2–9

LEARNING OBJECTIVES

1. To discuss the Old Testament background for Pentecost.

2. To discuss the role of the Holy Spirit in the Old Testament.

3. To discuss the role of the Holy Spirit after Pentecost.

QUOTATIONS

The New Testament church begins with the 120 who await the coming of the Holy Spirit. When he comes, he opens the floodgates by addressing Jews "from every nation under heaven" (v. 5). In all the different languages of these nations, the Holy Spirit through the mouths of his people presents the message of the wonders God has done. From these thousands of Jews who have come from numerous places, God adds three thousand to his church. God's truth is no longer confined to the city of Jerusalem. On the day of Pentecost, the church becomes worldwide.

—Simon Kistemaker

LECTURE OUTLINE

A. The day of Pentecost was a significant event in the history of redemption closely connected to the ascension.

1. "Touching His human nature Jesus is no longer present with us. Touching His divine nature He is never absent from us" (Christian creed).

2. Jesus promised not to leave His disciples comfortless, but promised to send His Spirit to them so that He would be with them until the end of the age.

B. "When the day of Pentecost arrived, they were all together in one place. And suddenly there came from heaven a sound like a mighty rushing wind, and it filled the entire house where they were sitting. And divided tongues as of fire appeared to them and rested on each one of them. And they were all filled with the Holy Spirit and began to speak in other tongues as the Spirit gave them utterance. Now there were dwelling in Jerusalem Jews, devout men from every nation under heaven. And at this sound the multitude came together, and they were bewildered, because each one was hearing them speak in his won language. And they were amazed and astonished, saying, 'Are not all these who are speaking Galileans? And how is it that we hear each of us in his own native language? . . .' And all were amazed and perplexed, saying to one another, 'What does this mean?' But others mocking said, 'They are filled with new wine'" (Acts 2:1–10, 12–13).
   - People were amazed because they could understand foreign languages as their own language.

C. "But Peter, standing with the eleven, lifted up his voice and addressed them, 'Men of Judea and all who dwell in Jerusalem, let this be known to you, and give ear to my words. For these men are not drunk, as you suppose, since it is only the third hour of the day. But this is what was uttered through the prophet Joel: "And in the last days it shall be, God declares, that I will pour out my Spirit on all flesh"'" (Acts 2:14–17a).
   - In order to understand the supernatural phenomenon that occurred at Pentecost it is necessary to examine the Old Testament.

D. "And the people complained in the hearing of the LORD about their misfortunes, and when the LORD heard it, his anger was kindled, and the fire of the LORD burned among them and consumed some outlying parts of the camp. Then the people cried out to Moses, and Moses prayed to the LORD, and the fire died down" (Num. 11:1–2).

- The Israelites begin to complain about their circumstances in the wilderness.

E. "Now the rabble that was among them had a strong craving. And the people of Israel also wept again and said, 'Oh that we had meat to eat! We remember the fish we ate in Egypt that cost nothing, the cucumbers, the melons, the leeks, the onions, and the garlic. But now our strength is dried up, and there is nothing at all but this manna to look at.' Now the manna was like coriander seed, and its appearance like that of bdellium. The people went about and gathered it and ground it in handmills or beat it in mortars and boiled it in pots and made cakes of it. And the taste of it was like the taste for cakes baked with oil. When the dew fell upon the camp in the night, the manna fell with it" (Num. 11:4–9).
  1. God provided the large body of Israelites that came out of Egypt with manna in the wilderness to eat.

  2. The Israelites begin to rebel in their hearts by longing for the foods they ate in Egypt even though they had lived in slavery there.

F. "Moses heard the people weeping throughout their clans, everyone at the door of his tent. And the anger of the Lord blazed hotly, and Moses was displeased" (Num. 11:10).
  - God was angry that Israel had forgotten that He had led them out of Egypt in love with a mighty hand.

G. "Moses said to the Lord, 'Why have you dealt ill with your servant? And why have I not found favor in your sight, that you lay the burden of all this people on me? Did I conceive all this people? Did I give them birth, that you should say to me, "Carry them in your bosom, as a nurse carries a nursing child," to the land that you swore to give their fathers? Where am I to get meat to give to all this people? For they weep before me and say "Give us meat, that we may eat"'" (Num. 11:11–13).
  - Sometimes Israel's leadership became so frustrated with the people that they asked God to take their life to be rid of them.

H. "I am not able to carry all this people alone; the burden is too heavy for me. If you will treat me like this, kill me at once, if I find favor in your sight, that I may not see my wretchedness" (Num. 11:14–15).
  - Moses asks God to take his life rather than to lead the people anymore.

I. "Then the Lord said to Moses, 'Gather for me seventy men of the elders of Israel, whom you know to be the elders of the people and officers over them, and bring them to the tent of meeting, and let them take their stand there with you. And I will come down and talk with you there. And I will take some of the Spirit that is on you and put it on them, and they shall bear the burden of the people with you, so that you may not bear it yourself alone. And say to the people, "Consecrate yourselves for tomorrow, and you shall eat meat, for you have wept in the hearing of the Lᴏʀᴅ, saying, 'Who will give us meat to eat?'"'" (Num. 11:16–18a).

1. Moses was the mediator of the Old Covenant and a charismatic leader.

2. Moses' leadership was exercised over the people by the power of God through an anointing of the Holy Spirit.

3. Old Testament believers enjoyed many of the benefits of the Holy Spirit.

4. Leaders had a special anointing of the Spirit that empowered them for ministry.

5. Kings were anointed, prophets were inspired, and priests were consecrated all to symbolize the power of the Spirit.

6. God decides to spread out the spirit that was upon Moses to the other leaders of Israel.

7. At Pentecost the Spirit is spread even further to the whole community of believers.

J. "And say to the people, 'Consecrate yourselves for tomorrow, and you shall eat meat, for you have wept in the hearing of the Lord, saying, "Who will give us meat to eat? For it was better for us in Egypt." Therefore the Lᴏʀᴅ will give you meat, and you shall eat. You shall not eat just one day, or two days, or five days, or ten days, or twenty days, but a whole month, until it comes out at your nostrils and becomes loathsome to you, because you have rejected the Lᴏʀᴅ who is among you and have wept before him, saying, "Why did we come out of Egypt?"'" (Num. 11:18–20).
   • God will punish the Israelites with such an abundance of meat that they will quickly grow sick of it.

K. "But Moses said, 'The people among whom I am number six hundred thousand on foot, and you have said, "I will give them meat, that they may eat a whole month!" Shall flocks and herds be slaughtered for them, and be enough for them? Or shall all the fish of the sea be gathered together for them, and be enough for them?' And the Lord said to Moses, 'Is the Lᴏʀᴅ's hand shortened? Now you shall see whether my word will come true for you or not'" (Num. 11:21–23).
   • The Lord reminds Moses that nothing is too difficult for Him.

L. "So Moses went out and told the people the words of the LORD. And he gathered seventy men of the elders of the people and placed them around the tent. Then the LORD came down in the cloud and spoke to him, and took some of the Spirit that was on him and put it on the seventy elders. And as soon as the Spirit rested on them, they prophesied. But they did not continue doing it. Now two men remained in the camp, one named Eldad, and the other named Medad, and the Spirit rested on them. They were among those registered, but they had not gone out to the tent, and so they prophesied in the camp. And a young man ran and told Moses, 'Eldad and Medad are prophesying in the camp.' And Joshua the son of Nun, the assistant of Moses from his youth, said, 'My lord Moses, stop them'" (Num. 11:24–28).
   • The people realized that prophesying was an outward manifestation of the Spirit's anointing.

M. "But Moses said to him, 'Are you jealous for my sake? Would that all the LORD's people were prophets, that the Lord would put his Spirit on them!'" (Num. 11:29).
   1. This prayer of Moses later became a prophecy written down by the prophet Joel.

   2. The Old Testament believers received the Spirit only as a temporary empowerment for ministry.

   3. At Pentecost all believers receive the Holy Spirit to dwell within them always.

   4. Every believer under the New Covenant has been empowered by God the Holy Spirit.

   5. All believers are empowered by the Spirit with gifts, but not all have the same gift.

   6. The New Testament church is a charismatic church in that it has been empowered by the Spirit with the gifts it needs to spread throughout the entire earth.

BIBLE STUDY

   1. What is the Old Testament background of Pentecost (see Deut. 16:9–12)? How does knowing this background make this day appropriate for the birth of the Christian church and the anointing of the Spirit?

2. Acts 2 makes clear the broad scope of the outpouring of the Holy Spirit, as well as the worldwide scope of the gospel's advance. In verses 4–11 and 21, what indications are given for this expansion of the work of the Holy Spirit and the gospel?

3. How do the events described during Pentecost show a reversal of the confusion of speech that occurred at the Tower of Babel (Gen. 11)? How are the blessings of these reversals continued in our day?

4. In Peter's sermon, he explained the signs they witnessed in terms of Old Testament prophecies being fulfilled in the work of Christ. What fulfillment of Joel's prophecy is described in verses 14–21? What fulfillment of David's prophecy is described in verse 22–39?

5. What is the reaction of the Sanhedrin to the preaching of Peter and John? How do Peter and John respond in Acts 4:19–20? How does this inform our practice of obedience toward those in authority over us?

DISCUSSION

1. In light of the Great Commission (Acts 1:8, Matt. 28:18–20), how does the event of Pentecost apply to your role in the ministry of the Christian church in our day?

2. How does Acts 2:23, 36 show the compatibility of God's sovereign purposes and human responsibility for their actions? Though Christ willingly offered Himself as a sacrifice, in what way are we personally responsible for His crucifixion?

3. How did the early believers give powerful testimony to the resurrection of Christ according to Acts 4:32–37? What actions can the church take today to give testimony to the resurrection of our Lord?

FOR FURTHER STUDY

Bruce, F.F. *The Book of Acts*
_____. *Paul: Apostle of the Heart Set Free*
Johnson, Dennis E. *The Message of Acts in the History of Redemption*

47

The Expansion of the Church

MESSAGE INTRODUCTION

The Acts of the Apostles could easily be given the title of the Acts of the Holy Spirit. The gift of the Holy Spirit's power at Pentecost sent shockwaves throughout the early church in Jerusalem and in surrounding regions. The Spirit empowered the apostles to preach the gospel in Judea, Samaria, and gradually throughout the ends of the earth. Such rapid expansion of the early church led to significant questions regarding the role of the Gentiles and the Mosaic law. Luke's account in Acts is the story of the Holy Spirit leading, guiding, and protecting Christ's church in its earliest years. In this lecture, Dr. Sproul discusses the expansion of the church.

SCRIPTURE READING

Acts 10–18

LEARNING OBJECTIVES

1. To emphasize the primacy of the Holy Spirit in the book of Acts.

2. To identify and describe the four primary groups in the early church.

3. To identify the pattern of growth of the early church.

QUOTATIONS

These twelve have seen and heard Jesus and now tell others about him (compare John 1:1). Filled with the Holy Spirit, they begin to proclaim the Good News in Jerusalem (see Luke 24:47). Then they preach the gospel in the Judean and Samarian countryside, and eventually they take it to Rome. Rome was the imperial capital from which all roads

extended, like spokes in a wheel, to the ends of the then-known world (cf. Isa. 5:26, "the
ends of the earth"). In the third gospel, Luke directs attention to Jerusalem, where
Jesus suffers, dies, rises from the dead, and ascends. In Acts, he focuses on Rome as the
destination of Christ's gospel. From Rome the Good News reaches the entire world.

—Simon Kistemaker

LECTURE OUTLINE

A. The Acts of the Apostles may be better entitled the Acts of the Holy Spirit.
   • The primary character in the book is the Holy Spirit who leads and guides
      the early church as it expands.

B. The book of Acts was written by Luke as the second volume in the history of Christ
    and the early church.

C. The book of Acts follows the outline of church expansion that Jesus detailed right
    before His ascension.
    1. "But you will receive power when the Holy Spirit has come upon you, and
        you will be my witnesses in Jerusalem and in all Judea and Samaria, and to
        the end of the earth" (Acts 1:8).

    2. Jerusalem is located in the center of Palestine.

    3. Jerusalem was located in the province of Judea.

    4. Samaria separated Judea in the south from Galilee in the north.

    5. The apostle Paul spreads the gospel to the Gentiles throughout the Roman
        world.

D. "And there arose on that day a great persecution against the church in Jerusalem,
    and they were all scattered throughout the regions of Judea and Samaria, except the
    apostles" (Acts 8:1b).
    • Persecution initially causes the church to scatter beyond Jerusalem.

E. "Now those who were scattered went about preaching the word" (Acts 8:4).
    • Common church members traveled to local regions teaching the Word of
       God.

F. Philip preached the Word in Samaria and encountered a sorcerer.
    1. "But there was a man named Simon, who had previously practiced magic
        in the city and amazed the people of Samaria, saying that he himself was
        somebody great. They all paid attention to him, from the least to the

greatest, saying, 'This man is the power of God that is called Great.' And they paid attention to him because for a long time he had amazed them with his magic. But when they believed Philip as he preached good news about the kingdom of God and the name of Jesus Christ, they were baptized, both men and women. Even Simon himself believed, and after being baptized he continued with Philip. And seeing signs and great miracles performed, he was amazed. Now when the apostles at Jerusalem heard that Samaria had received the Word of God, they sent to them Peter and John, who came down and prayed for them that they might receive the Holy Spirit, for he had not yet fallen on any of them, but they had only been baptized in the name of the Lord Jesus. Then they laid their hands on them and they received the Holy Spirit" (Acts 8:9–17).

  2. The gospel advances into Samaria to the great surprise of the Jerusalem church.

G. "At Caesarea there was a man named Cornelius, a centurion of what was known as the Italian Cohort, a devout man who feared God with all his household, gave alms generously to the people, and prayed continually to God" (Acts 10:1–2).
  • Cornelius, a Gentile, is identified as a god-fearer in Acts.

H. The early church had to face the question of how various groups would fit into the church.
  • The Jews, the Samaritans, the god-fearers, and the Gentiles were four groups that were a part of this debate.

I. The early church began with Jews at Pentecost.
  • The Jews filled with the Spirit at Pentecost became the nucleus of the first century church.

J. The Samaritans began to believe the gospel and be baptized even though the Jews had no dealings with Samaritans.
  • The apostles accepted them into the church and laid their hands on them so that they too received the Holy Spirit.

K. The god-fearers were Gentiles who had been partially converted to Judaism.
  1. The Jews required the god-fearers to adopt Jewish doctrines, undergo a purification bath, and be circumcised.

  2. Non-circumcised god-fearers were treated as second-class members of the community.

  3. Cornelius was a member of the god-fearers.

L. "So Peter opened his mouth and said: 'Truly I understand that God shows no par-
tiality, but in every nation anyone who fears him and does what is right is acceptable
to him. As for the word that he sent to Israel, preaching good news of peace through
Jesus Christ (he is Lord of all), you yourselves know what happened throughout
all Judea, beginning from Galilee after the baptism that John proclaimed: how God
anointed Jesus of Nazareth with the Holy Spirit and with power'" (Acts 10:34–38a).
   • Peter proceeds to summarize the life and ministry of Jesus.

M. "While Peter was still saying these things, the Holy Spirit fell on all who heard the
Word. And the believers from among the circumcised who had come with Peter
were amazed, because the gift of the Holy Spirit was poured out even on the Gentiles. For they were hearing them speaking in tongues and extolling God" (Acts
10:44–46a).
   1. A smaller version of Pentecost happens for the Gentiles to show their equal
      inclusion into the church.

   2. The Jews were shocked that uncircumcised Gentiles were receiving the gift
      of the Holy Spirit.

N. "Then Peter declared, 'Can anyone withhold water for baptizing these people, who
have received the Holy Spirit just as we have?' And he commanded them to be
baptized in the name of Jesus Christ. Then they asked him to remain for some days"
(Acts 10:46b–48).
   • Peter argued that if God did not withhold His Spirit from the Gentiles nei-
     ther should the church withhold baptism which was the sign of the New
     Covenant.

O. The gospel expands to the Jews, Samaritans, and god-fearers in the early chapters
of Acts and then is brought to the Gentiles by Paul in his missionary journeys.
   • The Ephesian believers also experience a form of Pentecost (Acts 19) to
     reveal God's inclusion of them into the church.

P. Luke details the story of the gospel reaching all four groups of people in the book of Acts.

Q. The fiercest question in the early church was regarding the inclusion of the Gentiles
into the church.
   • Christ became the hope of Israel and the Gentiles.

R. The Spirit goes before the apostles to open the eyes of the Jews, Samaritans, god-
fearers, and the Gentiles.
   1. Pentecost is an explosion of divine redemptive power on the world and church.

   2. The hidden mystery of God's church filled with His Spirit is unleashed on this day.

BIBLE STUDY

1. Why was the repentance of Cornelius so significant (Acts 10), and why does Peter feel compelled to explain his actions (chap. 11)?

2. What great natural calamity did the early church face in Jerusalem (Acts 11:27–30)? How did the early church address this crisis? How do their actions inform our own as the church in the world today?

3. How does Paul identify Jesus as the pivotal figure in Israel's history in his sermon at Pisidan Antioch (Acts 13:16–41)? What is his point in doing so?

4. What dispute leads to calling the Council of Jerusalem in Acts 15? How is the issue resolved? Why does the council cite Amos' imagery regarding the restoration to justify their decision (see Amos 9:11–12)?

5. Why are Paul and Silas accused of "turning the world upside down" in Acts 17:6? In what specific ways does the gospel turn the world upside down today?

6. How does Paul in his speech to the Athenians identify truths in their culture? How does he explain the fact that all truth is God's truth? How does he draw their attention to the truth in the gospel? Why did his hearers end up scoffing at him?

DISCUSSION

1. What is more difficult for you: to witness to your family and friends, or to a stranger? Why?

2. How are Gentile Christians urged to limit their freedom in Acts 15 for the sake of peace and unity with Jewish believers? Give an example of when it is necessary for one believer to limit his freedom for the sake of another believer.

3. Notice the unique signs and wonders that accompanied the apostolic preaching of the gospel throughout the book of Acts. How did this give credibility to the apostles' message and work in establishing the church?

FOR FURTHER STUDY

Bruce, F.F. *The Book of Acts*
_____. *Paul: Apostle of the Heart Set Free*
Johnson, Dennis E. *The Message of Acts in the History of Redemption*

48

The Conversion of Paul

MESSAGE INTRODUCTION

The office of the apostle held great authority in the early church. The men chosen for this position had to meet very specific requirements because the New Testament apostle was God's agent of revelation who proclaimed the Word of God. Paul did not meet some of the apostolic requirements the church established, but he did receive a direct and immediate call from Christ, which gave him apostolic authority. That famous call came on the Damascus road when God converted the great persecutor of the church into the Apostle to the Gentiles. In this lecture, Dr. Sproul discusses the conversion of Paul.

SCRIPTURE READING

Acts 19–28

LEARNING OBJECTIVES

1. To identify the requirements for being an apostle in the early church.

2. To describe the conversion of Saul on the road to Damascus.

3. To discuss the significance of Paul's conversion in his evangelism.

QUOTATIONS

No single event, apart from the Christ-event itself, has proved so determinant for the course of Christian history as the conversion and commissioning of Paul. For anyone who accepts Paul's own explanation of his Damascus-road experience, it would be difficult to disagree with the observation of an eighteenth-century writer that "the conversion and apostleship of St. Paul alone, duly considered, was of itself a demonstration sufficient to prove Christianity to be a divine revelation."

With no conscious preparation, Paul found himself instantaneously compelled by what he saw and heard to acknowledge that Jesus of Nazareth, the crucified one, was alive after his passion, vindicated and exalted by God, and was now conscripting him into his service. There could be no resistance to this compulsion, no kicking out against this goad which was driving him in the opposite direction to that which he had hitherto been pursuing. He capitulated forthwith to the commands of this new master; a conscript he might be, but henceforth also a devoted and lifelong volunteer.

—F.F. Bruce

LECTURE OUTLINE

A. Luke possibly wrote the book of Acts to give the church a defense of the apostleship of Paul.

B. Matthias was chosen by the other apostles to replace Judas who had committed suicide after he betrayed Christ.

C. There were three requirements established for apostleship.
    1. The individual first had to be a disciple.

    2. The individual had to be an eyewitness of the resurrection.

    3. The individual needed to have a direct call from Christ.

D. The prophets of the Old Testament competed with the false prophets to proclaim the truth.
    1. An important test for a prophet in the Old Testament was his ability to articulate the circumstances of his call by God to the prophetic office.

    2. Isaiah, Jeremiah, Ezekiel, and Amos are zealous to record the events surrounding their call to the prophetic office.

E. The apostles of the New Testament occupy an office that parallels the office of the prophet in the Old Testament.
    1. The New Testament apostle is God's agent of revelation who proclaims the Word of God.

    2. Paul was not a disciple or an eyewitness of the resurrection in the same manner as the other apostles.

F. Paul did receive a direct and immediate call from Christ, which gave him apostolic authority.

- The apostolic authority was confirmed by the other known apostles although his authority came from Christ Himself.

G. "But Saul, still breathing threats and murder against the disciples of the Lord, went to the high priest and asked him for letters to the synagogues at Damascus, so that if he found any belonging to the Way, men or women, he might bring them bound to Jerusalem" (Acts 9:1–2).

1. Paul had a reputation in the Christian church as a scourge of the Christian community.

2. Paul had studied under Gamaliel who was the leading teacher of his day and was the Pharisee of Pharisees.

3. Luke gives a detailed account of Saul's conversion in Acts 9 in order to show how God transformed him from a persecutor of the church to an apostle of the church.

H. "Now as he went on his way, he approached Damascus, and suddenly a light from heaven flashed around him. And falling to the ground he heard a voice saying to him, 'Saul, Saul, why are you persecuting me?'" (Acts 9:3–4).

1. Saul was blinded by the shining light of God's glory.

2. The Lord repeats Saul's name twice as a sign of intimacy.

3. Saul is not asked why he persecutes the church, but rather Christ Himself because the church is the body of Christ.

4. Anyone who assaults the church assaults Christ Himself.

I. "And he said, 'Who are you, Lord?' And he said, 'I am Jesus, whom you are persecuting'" (Acts 9:5).

1. Goads were attached to carts to prompt oxen to move forward.

2. Paul was kicking against the goads by attacking the church of God.

J. "'But rise and enter the city, and you will be told what you are to do.' The men who were traveling with him stood speechless, hearing the voice but seeing no one. Saul rose from the ground, and although his eyes were opened, he saw nothing. So they led him by the hand and brought him into Damascus. And for three days he was without sight, and neither ate nor drank. Now there was a disciple at Damascus named Ananias. The Lord said to him in a vision, 'Ananias.' And he said, 'Here I am, Lord.' And the Lord said to him, 'Rise and go to the street called Straight, and at the house of Judas look for a man of Tarsus named Saul, for behold, he is praying, and he has seen in a vision a man named Ananias come in and lay his hands on him so that he might regain his sight.' But Ananias answered, 'Lord, I have heard from many about this man, how much evil he has done to your saints at Jerusalem. And here he has authority from the chief priests to bind all who call on your name'" (Acts 9:6–14).

- Ananias reacts in fear to God's command to go meet Saul.

K. "But the Lord said to him, 'Go, for he is a chosen instrument of mine to carry my name before the Gentiles and kings and the children of Israel. For I will show him how much he must suffer for the sake of my name'" (Acts 9:15–16).

1. Paul frequently referenced his conversion and his calling to preach the gospel and suffer for the name of Christ.

2. Paul used the story of his conversion in his testimony before King Agrippa in Acts 26.

3. Paul was obedient to the call placed on his life until the day he was beheaded by Emperor Nero in Rome.

BIBLE STUDY

1. Saul (later to be renamed "Paul") was an accomplice to the stoning of Stephen (Acts 7:58) and had persecuted the disciples of Christ with great zeal. How does Acts 8:1, 3 and 9:1–2 give us insight into his pre-conversion character? Why do you suppose Saul took this initiative in persecuting Christians?

2. In Acts 9:3–5, who appeared to Saul on the road to Damascus? In verses 5–8, how did his disposition and plans begin to change? What had he gotten theologically wrong up to this point?

3. What purposes of God for Saul's conversion are revealed in verses 15 and 16? How were these predictions fulfilled later in Paul's ministry (Acts 22:21; 25:13)?

4. Moving on to the ministry of Paul in Acts 19, how does he engage in spiritual warfare in Ephesus? Why does Paul experience victory over the powers of darkness and the sons of Sceva experience defeat? How or why does this serve to extol the name of the Lord Jesus (v. 17)?

5. What miracle does Paul perform in Troas (Acts 20:7–12)? What is the common message in each of the following stories (1 Kings 17:17–24; Luke 8:40–56; Acts 9:36–43)? What purpose do these miraculous events serve?

6. What were the charges for which Paul was arrested in Acts 21:27–29? In what sense were the charges true, and in what sense were they false?

DISCUSSION

1. Comparing Acts 9, verses 1 and 4, we see that persecuting Jesus' disciples is the same as persecuting Jesus. What does this say about the way Jesus views His church? How does this apply to any persecution that we experience as His disciples?

2. Acts 9:31, 35, and 42 refer to the continuing multiplication of the church. In addition to the unique miracles performed by Christ through the apostles in the latter two verses, what four characteristics of the church are identified in verse 31 as accompanying the multiplication of the church? How can you apply these characteristics in your own life? In your church?

3. What are Paul's circumstances in Rome at the end of the book of Acts? How does he endeavor to take advantage of his circumstances for the sake of the gospel?

FOR FURTHER STUDY

Bruce, F.F. *The Book of Acts*
_____. *Paul: Apostle of the Heart Set Free*
Johnson, Dennis E. *The Message of Acts in the History of Redemption*

49

Romans

MESSAGE INTRODUCTION

The book of Romans is one of the most treasured and studied books of the Pauline corpus. God has used this great epistle in the lives of many of His followers to bring repentance and faith. Some of those who have been so influenced are men such as St. Augustine, Martin Luther, and John Wesley. The apostle Paul explores the depths of human wickedness, God's gracious initiative, and the consequences of His endless love for His people in this systematic presentation of the gospel. In this lecture, Dr. Sproul discusses the book of Romans.

SCRIPTURE READING

Romans

LEARNING OBJECTIVES

1. To appreciate the significance of the book of Romans in church history.

2. To outline Paul's presentation of the gospel in the book of Romans.

3. To discuss the practical implications of the gospel for daily living.

QUOTATIONS

It is commonly agreed that the "Epistle to the Romans" is one of the greatest Christian writings. Its power has been demonstrated again and again at critical points in the history of the Christian church. Augustine of Hippo, for example, was converted through reading a passage from this letter, and thus began a period of the greatest importance for the church. It is not too much to say that at a later time Martin Luther's spiritual experience was shaped by his coming to grips with what Paul says in this epistle. The Reformation may be regarded as the unleashing of new spiritual life as a result of a renewed understanding of the teaching of Romans. Again, John Wesley's conversion was triggered by hearing Luther's Preface to Romans *read, a preface, of course, inspired by the epistle. Nearer to our own day it was Karl Barth's coming to grips with the message of the book that ended an era of sterile liberalism and ushered in a more fruitful period of biblical theology. But Romans is not for great minds only. The humble believer also finds inspiration and direction in these pages. Romans is not an easy book. But it has always yielded rich dividends to anyone who has taken the time to study it seriously, and it does so still.*

—Leon Morris

LECTURE OUTLINE

A. Great theologians have been one of God's great gifts to the church.
   1. St. Augustine, Thomas Acquinas, Martin Luther, John Calvin, and Jonathan Edwards were men of great learning, deep faith, and passionate devotion to the Word of God.

   2. These great theologians would all agree that the apostle Paul was the greatest theologian that ever lived.

B. Paul was not just a great thinker, but also a missionary, pastor, and an evangelist.
   • He had a great understanding, a pastor's heart, and a passionate zeal to win people to Christ.

C. Many theologians believe the book of Romans is Paul's magnum opus and his attempt to succinctly put forth the whole counsel of God regarding salvation.
   1. The book of Romans was instrumental in the conversions of St. Augustine, Martin Luther, and John Wesley.

   2. Romans was known in the sixteenth century as the book of the Reformation.

D. The central theme of Romans that Paul discusses is the imputation of God's righteousness by faith.
E. Paul establishes the universality of man's guilt in the opening chapters of the epistle.
   1. All of mankind stand before God's righteous tribunal and are declared guilty.

   2. Justification by faith is the only avenue of salvation for the unjust.

F. Paul explains that God has revealed Himself to everyone through the creation, and therefore, none can claim ignorance of the Almighty.

1. The universal response of the human race to God's general revelation is to suppress, stifle, and corrupt His revelation into some form of idolatry.

2. All humans tend to worship the creature or creation rather than the Creator Himself.

3. Mankind has also ignored God's inner revelation or human conscience regarding right and wrong.

4. Jews disobeyed the written Law of God, despite having it written down for them in Scripture.

5. All men, Jews and Gentiles, have fallen short of the glory of God.

6. By the works of the law no man will be justified because no man obeys the law completely.

G. But now a different righteousness is revealed from heaven which is the righteousness of God given to those who have faith in Christ.
   1. Abraham is given as an example of one who was declared to be righteous by faith aside from any works.

   2. Those who are justified have peace with God and have access into His presence.

   3. The journey of sanctification immediately begins for the justified.

H. The life of the believer is a battle to put to death the works of the flesh and to walk in the new life of the Spirit.

I. "And we know that for those who love God all things work together for good, for those who are called according to his purpose" (Rom. 8:28).

J. Paul explains the theme of divine election in chapters 9–11.
   1. Paul uses Jacob as an example who was chosen for the kingdom of God on the basis of God's election and not on Jacob's works.

   2. It is the divine prerogative to give or withhold mercy according to the good pleasure of God's counsel.

K. Paul breaks into praise and doxology as he contemplates the depths of God's mercy and love.

L. Paul discusses the role of gospel preaching as God's means for saving the world in chapter 10.
    •   Believers are blessed to be participants in expanding the kingdom of God.

M. Paul discusses the role and hope of Israel and his people's reaction to the gospel in chapter 11.

N. The remaining chapters of Romans focus on the practical implications of the gospel for daily living.

O. Believers are encouraged to have their minds transformed, to pray without ceasing, and to be charitable to others.
    •   Believers are to submit to authorities because they are established by God.

P. Paul closes his epistle to the Romans with personal greetings to many of those he knew in the Roman church.

Q. The book of Romans is simple enough for a child's understanding and yet can keep the greatest theologians busy for a lifetime.

BIBLE STUDY

1. What can all people learn from creation according to Romans 1:19? But how do all fallen people respond to the general revelation of God? What is God's response to such people according to Romans 1:24–32?

2. The key verses of the first chapter of Romans are 16–17. If the gospel is the power of God towards those who believe, does that limit its effects to the non-Christian? How is the gospel the power of God in the life of the believer?

3. How does Paul expose the self-righteous elitism of the Jews in Romans 2? How does Paul define the true servant of God's kingdom in verse 29?

4. How does Paul seek to challenge his readers' thinking on such topics as the law, righteousness, justice, faith, and sin in Romans 3:21–31?

5. Make a list of the gifts we have been given if we have faith in Christ according to Romans 5:1–11. According to verses 12–21, what was imputed to us in Adam? What was imputed to us in Christ?

6. What is the stumbling block over which the Jews stumbled in their quest for salvation? How are both Jews and Gentiles saved according to Romans 10? What needs to happen for people to call on the Lord according to verses 14–15?

DISCUSSION

1. Read Romans 7. What was the power the law had on an individual before that person received God's grace? How does Paul describe sin as his behavior and not his primary identity in verses 14–25? Is this a good description of you today?

2. What is the analogy Paul gives in Romans 11 to explain how the Gentiles became part of the people of God? What warning does he give them regarding unbelief?

3. How do Romans 12 and 14 show us the practical implications of our justification in regards to our daily work, thoughts, gifts, relationships, and enemies?

4. Why does Paul command believers to live in obedience to authorities in Romans 13? How does the command to love summarize our obligations to God and others according to this chapter?

FOR FURTHER STUDY

Moo, Douglas. *The Epistle to the Romans*
Sproul, R.C. *Romans* (St. Andrew's Expositional Commentary)

50

1 and 2 Corinthians

MESSAGE INTRODUCTION

The city of Corinth was one of the greatest commercial and entertainment centers on the Grecian peninsula. The city was also known throughout the ancient world as a center of prostitution and licentiousness. A struggling church was established here by the apostle Paul on his second missionary journey. Yet it was not long before the apostle heard disturbing reports about the Corinthian congregation. The church had splintered into several factions and had become divided over such issues as church discipline, food sacrificed to idols, tongues, and the resurrection. The Apostle to the Gentiles wrote words to the Corinthians to guide and instruct that are still important for the church today. In this lecture, Dr. Sproul discusses 1 and 2 Corinthians.

SCRIPTURE READING

1 and 2 Corinthians

LEARNING OBJECTIVES

1. To identify the commercial and geographical significance of Corinth on the Grecian Peninsula.

2. To summarize Paul's instructions regarding the problems in the church at Corinth.

3. To discuss Paul's defense of his ministry in 2 Corinthians.

QUOTATIONS

Corinth was the biggest city Paul had yet encountered, a brash new commercial metropolis. . . . It squeezed nearly a quarter of a million people into a comparatively small area, a large proportion being slaves engaged in the unending movement of goods. Slaves or free, Corinthians were rootless, cut off from their country background, drawn from races and districts all over the empire ... a curiously close parallel to the population of a twentieth-century "inner-city." ...

Paul had seen the Christian churched grow and flourish in the moderately-sized cities he had found in Macedonia. If the love of Christ Jesus could take root in Corinth, the most populated, wealthy, commercial-minded and sex-obsessed city of Eastern Europe, it must prove powerful anywhere.

—J.C. Pollock

LECTURE OUTLINE

A. Paul was the Apostle to the Gentiles, an extraordinary pastor, and a profound theologian.

B. Paul was also a task theologian who could apply the deep truths of theology to the unique problems of the early church.
   1. Paul wrote letters to deal with the real problems churches encountered.

   2. Paul wrote about Christ's return to the church in Thessalonica and the confusion of the Judaizers to the Galatians.

C. The epistles of the New Testament are generally arranged according to length from the longest to the shortest.

D. Paul received very troubling reports about the church in Corinth during his third missionary journey.
   1. The early church was not as pure and pious as we often believe.

   2. The infant church was often immature and ignorant of the things of God.

   3. The letters from Christ to His infant church in the book of Revelation are generally not complimentary.

E. One of the most troubled churches from the beginning was the church in Corinth.
   1. The city of Corinth built by the Romans was the commercial, entertainment, and immorality capital of the Grecian peninsula.

   2. The Corinth of Paul's day had a population of 500,000 people.

   3. Corinth was known internationally as a licentious city full of prostitution and idolatry.

   4. Paul and Apollos were significant leaders in the church at Corinth.

F. The Corinthian church was riddled with corruption and confusion.
    1. The church was divided by factions and groups paying allegiance to individual leaders.

    2. One church member was having a very public incestuous relationship with his father's wife and he was not being disciplined by the elders of the church.

    3. Christians were taking other Christians to court for lawsuits.

    4. The celebration of the Lord's Supper was being abused in the church at Corinth.

G. Paul gives a brilliant exposition of the identity of the church to address many of the problems in Corinth.

H. Paul discusses the role of charismatic gifts in the church because they were being abused by the church in Corinth.
    • The primary point of 1 Corinthians 13 is that the gifts of the Spirit should only be exercised in love for the mutual edification of the entire church body.

I. The apostles received their authority from Christ Himself and established churches in which they appointed elders and deacons.
    • The apostles did not appoint additional apostles.

J. Gifted teachers and leaders in Corinth were claiming apostolic authority apart from the church government originally established by Christ's apostle.
    1. Individuals claimed authority and precedence over others on the basis of the alleged superiority of their spiritual gift.

    2. Paul wrote at least two, probably three, and possibly four or five letters to the church in Corinth to discuss unity in the body of Christ.

    3. Many scholars have unsuccessfully attempted to locate the "harsh letter" that Paul wrote to Corinth and refers to in the rest of his Corinthian correspondence.

K. Many of the issues Paul addressed in his letters to Corinth were not resolved immediately and continued to linger for decades.
    • Near the end of the first century, Clement, the bishop of Rome, exhorted the Corinthian church to read again the letters Paul wrote to them many years earlier.

L. A debate surrounding the resurrection of Christ was one of the most serious controversies in the Corinthian church.

   1. Paul gives a spirited defense of the resurrection of Christ in 1 Corinthians 15.

   2. The great hope for the Christian is his participation in the resurrection of Christ.

   3. Paul explores what it would mean if Christ had not risen from the grave and concludes that believers would be the most miserable of men if Christ has not risen.

   4. Paul affirms the resurrection of the dead by stating that corruptible and mortal bodies will be changed at their resurrection into incorruptible and immortal bodies.

M. Second Corinthians is Paul's most personal and autobiographical letter.

N. Paul is drawn into a defense of his ministry by his critics.

   1. "I wish you would bear with me in a little foolishness. Do bear with me! I feel a divine jealousy for you, for I betrothed you to one husband, to present you as a pure virgin to Christ. But I am afraid that as the serpent deceived Eve by his cunning, your thoughts will be led astray from a sincere and pure devotion to Christ. . . . I consider that I am not in the least inferior to these super-apostles. Even if I am unskilled in speaking, I am not so in knowledge; indeed, in every way we have made this plain to you in all things. Or did I commit a sin in humbling myself so that you might be exalted, because I preached God's gospel to you free of charge? . . . I repeat, let no one think me foolish. But even if you do, accept me as a fool, so that I too may boast a little" (2 Cor. 11:1–3, 5–7).

   2. Paul took a moment to boast about his credentials as an apostle against those who claimed to be super-apostles in Corinth.

   3. "Are they Hebrews? So am I. Are they Israelites? So am I. Are they offspring of Abraham? So am I. Are they servants of Christ? I am a better one—I am talking like a madman—with far greater labors, far more imprisonments, with countless beatings, and often near death. Five times I received at the hands of the Jews the forty lashes less one. Three times I was beaten with rods. Once I was stoned. Three times I was shipwrecked; a night and a day I was adrift at sea; on frequent journeys, in danger from rivers, danger from robbers, danger from my own people, danger from Gentiles, danger in the city, danger in the wilderness, danger at sea, danger from false brothers; in

toil and hardship, through many a sleepless night, in hunger and thirst, often without food, in cold and exposure. And, apart from other things, there is the daily pressure on me of my anxiety for all the churches. Who is weak, and I am not weak? Who is made to fall, and I am not indignant? If I must boast, I will boast of the things that show my weakness. The God and Father of the Lord Jesus, he who is blessed forever, knows that I am not lying. At Damascus, the governor under King Aretas was guarding the city of Damascus in order to seize me, but I was let down in a basket through a window in the wall and escaped his hands" (2 Cor. 11:22–33).

4. Paul is not bragging about his conquests, but rather saying he has poured himself out intellectually, spiritually, emotionally, and physically for the Corinthians.

5. Paul sets out a defense of his ministry before his critics, and says judge me from my labor.

BIBLE STUDY

1. What was the basis of the divisions in the church at Corinth? How does Paul attack the nature of these divisions by discussing the foolishness of the cross?

2. What immorality does Paul rebuke in the church at Corinth in 1 Corinthians 5? How does Paul want the Corinthian church leaders to handle this sin?

3. How does Paul refute the idea in the Corinthian church that our physical bodies do not matter and therefore neither does sexual immorality (see 1 Cor. 6:9–20)? How does Paul link worship, freedom, and obedience in this passage?

4. What stern warning regarding the Lord's Supper does Paul give in 1 Corinthians 11:17–34? How does Paul counsel the Corinthians regarding their approach to the Lord's Supper in this passage?

DISCUSSION

1. How does Paul define love in 1 Corinthians 13? How does contemporary culture define love? How does Paul's emphasis on love speak to the various issues in the Corinthian church? In your church?

2. Read 1 Corinthians 15. What are the consequences for believers if there is no resurrection of the body? What are the details Paul gives regarding the resurrection body believers will receive upon Christ's return?

3. What does Paul teach about the heart of a giver under the New Testament in 2 Corinthians 9:6–10? How will God respond to a faithful giver?

FOR FURTHER STUDY

Barnett, Paul. *The Second Epistle to the Corinthians*
Hodge, Charles. *1 & 2 Corinthians*
Morris, Leon. *1 Corinthians*

51

Prison Epistles

MESSAGE INTRODUCTION

The apostle Paul endured a lifetime of persecution and periods of imprisonment. Yet even as he suffered for proclaiming the gospel, the apostle still contributed to the growth of the church by writing letters to the congregations of the first century. Four of these letters written from prison have been designated collectively as the Prison Epistles. The apostle's letters to the Ephesians, Philippians, Colossians, and Philemon contain some of Paul's richest theology and best wisdom for godly living. In this lecture, Dr. Sproul discusses the Prison Epistles.

SCRIPTURE READING

Galatians, Ephesians, Philippians, Colossians, Philemon

LEARNING OBJECTIVES

1. To discuss the significance of Paul's call to continual rejoicing in his epistle to the Philippians.

2. To identify the role of the cosmic Christ theme in Paul's letter to the Colossians.

3. To discuss Paul's doctrine of the church in his epistle to the Ephesians.

QUOTATIONS

The outcome of the period of imprisonment is not difficult to assess, even though there may be some questions as to whether Paul was released or not. In spite of his confinement at Caesarea and at Rome, Paul's ministry was not ended. Through his assistants and friends, who are mentioned in the salutations of his epistles, he maintained constant communication with contemplation, out of which came the priceless revelation of the Prison Epistles. His appeal to Caesar brought Christianity directly to the attention of the Roman government and compelled the civil authorities to pass judgment on its legality. . . . In the decade of the Gentile mission from AD 46 to 56, and in the four years of Paul's imprisonment, the church came out from under the banner of Judaism and formed its own ranks as an independent movement. It was now ready for even greater advances in missionary expansion.

—Merrill C. Tenney

LECTURE OUTLINE

A. The apostle Paul endured a lifetime of persecution and periods of imprisonment.

B. Paul wrote four letters during one of these imprisonments that have been designated collectively as the Prison Epistles.
    - Ephesians, Philippians, Colossians, and Philemon are known as the "Prison Epistles."

C. Philippians is known as the "Epistle of Joy" because of Paul's emphasis on rejoicing despite one's circumstances.
    1. Joy is one of the fruits of the Spirit that should be evident in every believer's life.

    2. Believers suffer the tribulations of this world, but still have lives characterized by joy.

    3. Paul expressed a contagious joy regardless of his circumstances and called the Philippians to do the same.

    4. The Philippians are urged to rejoice because the One who began the redemptive work in their souls will be faithful to complete it.

D. "For to me to live is Christ, and to die is gain. If I am to live in the flesh, that means fruitful labor for me. Yet which I shall choose I cannot tell. I am hard pressed between the two. My desire is to depart and be with Christ, for that is far better. But to remain in the flesh is more necessary on your account" (Phil. 1:21–24).
    1. Paul longed to depart and be with Christ, but he also longed to continue ministering to the churches.

    2. Paul did not label this current life as entirely bad, but he knew the life to come would be even better.

E. "Have this mind among yourselves, which is yours in Christ Jesus, who, though he was in the form of God, did not count equality with God a thing to be grasped, but made himself nothing, taking the form of a servant, being born in the likeness of men. And being found in human form, he humbled himself by becoming obedient to the point of death, even death on a cross. Therefore God has highly exalted him and bestowed on him the name that is above every name, so that at the name of Jesus every knee should bow, in heaven and on earth and under the earth, and every tongue confess that Jesus Christ is Lord, to the glory of God the Father" (Phil. 2:5–11).

   1.   The Christian church is called to emulate Christ in His humility.

   2.   Christ emptied Himself of His prerogatives and dignity and became a servant on our behalf.

F. "But whatever gain I had, I counted as loss for the sake of Christ. Indeed, I count everything as loss because of the surpassing worth of knowing Christ Jesus my Lord. For his sake I have suffered the loss of all things and count them as rubbish, in order that I may gain Christ and be found in him, not having a righteousness of my own that comes from the law, but that which comes through faith in Christ, the righteousness from God that depends on faith—that I may know him and the power of his resurrection, and may share his sufferings, becoming like him in his death, that by any means possible I may attain the resurrection from the dead. Not that I have already obtained this or am already perfect, but I press on to make it my own, because Christ Jesus has made me his own. Brothers, I do not consider that I have made it my own. But one thing I do: for getting what lies behind and straining forward to what lies ahead, I press on toward the goal for the prize of the upward call of God in Christ Jesus" (Phil. 3:7–14).

   1.   "The chief business of the Christian is to press into the kingdom of God." —Jonathan Edwards

   2.   Paul is focused on moving away from the past and towards maturity in the kingdom of God.

G. The Epistle to the Colossians has received less attention in the church, but is one of Paul's great masterpieces.

   1.   The Colossians were in danger of a heretical invasion and conquest by an early form of Gnosticism.

   2.   The Gnostics were a group of mystics who believed that they had special knowledge regarding spiritual things.

   3.   Gnosticism was a syncretistic religion comprised of elements of Oriental philosophy, Dualistic religion, Greek philosophy, and Christian belief.

4. Gnostics believed Jesus was more like an angel than a son of God, and they were involved in the worship of angels.

5. In order to combat this heresy, Paul emphasizes the supremacy of Christ over all other beings.

H. Colossians is a revelation of the cosmic Christ who is not just the redeemer of men or the Jewish Messiah, but the very expression or God Himself and the Lord of the universe.

1. "He is the image of the invisible God, the firstborn of all creation. For by him all things were created, in heaven and on earth, visible and invisible, whether thrones or dominions or rulers or authorities—all things were created through him and for him" (Col. 1:15–16).

2. The universe was created by Him, for Him, and is held together through Him.

3. The Christian faith cannot be compartmentalized and privatized, but must always acknowledge the cosmic supremacy of Christ.

4. Paul knew proclaiming the authority of Christ would result in suffering, but he also knew participating in Christ's sufferings would mean participating in Christ's resurrection life.

I. Paul probably wrote the Epistle to the Ephesians as a circular letter which would be read in several different congregations.

1. Ephesians reviews many of the themes found in Romans.

2. Paul discusses the nature of the church as the body of Christ and as the company of the elect.

J. The doctrine of predestination is discussed by Paul in his letter to the Ephesians.

1. "Blessed be the God and Father of our Lord Jesus Christ, who has blessed us in Christ with every spiritual blessing in the heavenly places, even as he chose us in him before the foundation of the world, that we should be holy and blameless before him. In love he predestined us for adoption through Jesus Christ, according to the purpose of his will, to the praise of his glorious grace, with which he has blessed us in the Beloved" (Eph. 1:3–6).

2. God's elects His people unto salvation according to the good pleasure of His will.

3. God's plan of predestination for believers was established before the foundation of the earth and was accomplished entirely by God's grace.

4. "And you were dead in the trespasses and sins in which you once walked, following the course of this world, following the prince of the power of the air, the spirit that is now at work in the sons of disobedience—among whom we all once lived in the passions of our flesh, carrying out the desires of the body and the mind, and were by nature children of wrath, like the rest of mankind. But God, being rich in mercy, because of the great love with which he loved us, even when we were dead in our trespasses, made us alive together with Christ—by grace you have been saved—and raised us up with him and seated us with him in the heavenly places in Christ Jesus, so that in the coming ages he might show the immeasurable riches of his grace in kindness toward us in Christ Jesus. For by grace you have been saved through faith. And this is not your own doing, it is the gift of God, not a result of works, so that no one may boast. For we are his workmanship, created in Christ Jesus for good works, which God prepared beforehand, that we should walk in them" (Eph. 2:1–10).

K. Paul describes the life of the Christian in the latter chapters of Ephesians and what it means to be imitators of God and to walk in the Spirit.
1. Paul describes the practical implications of the gospel for the husband-wife, parent-child, and master-slave relationship.

2. Paul alerts the Ephesians to the threatening schemes of the Evil One.

3. Believers are to put on the full armor of God in their efforts to stand firm against the Devil's attacks and be imitators of God.

BIBLE STUDY

1. What do those who try to earn their salvation lose according to Paul in Galatians 3:1–5? What was the somewhat unexpected purpose of the law revealed here?

2. How can we live our lives differently because we have become sons rather than slaves (cf. Gal. 3:24–4:7)? How had the Galatians lost their spirit of joy according to Galatians 4:15?

3. How does alienation characterize those who are outside of Christ (Eph. 2:11–12)? How does the work of Christ bring oneness and peace (Eph. 2:13–18)? What are the three metaphors Paul uses to describe God's people in Ephesians 2:19–22?

4. How does being a member of God's kingdom change the relationship between spouses (Eph. 5:21–33), children and parents (Eph. 6:1–4), and slaves and masters (Eph. 6:5–9)? How does our relationship with the Devil and evil forces change (Eph. 2:2–3; 6:10–20)? Why is each piece of the armor of God necessary for our warfare?

5. Read Philippians 3. How does Paul define true joy? How does Paul warn the Philippians about the threats to their joy? Why does Paul warn against legalism (vs. 2–3) and license (vs. 18–19) in this chapter?

DISCUSSION

1. Why is Paul so thankful and joyful about the Philippians in chapter one? What common experiences did they both share? Who do you have a similar relationship with in your life?

2. What are the reasons why Christians should reject legalism according to Colossians 2:6–23? Why is legalism ineffective for growth and sanctification?

3. What request does Paul make of Philemon regarding the slave Onesimus? How does forgiveness and redemption characterize this story? In what ways do you imagine this letter was countercultural in Paul's day?

FOR FURTHER STUDY

Bruce, F.F. *The Epistles to the Colossians, to Philemon, and to the Ephesians*
Fung, Ronald Y.K. *The Epistle to the Galatians*
Luther, Martin. *Galatians*
O'Brien, Peter T. *The Epistle to the Philippians*
O'Brien, Peter T. *The Letter to the Ephesians*
Sproul, R.C. *The Purpose of God: An Exposition of Ephesians*

52

1 and 2 Timothy

MESSAGE INTRODUCTION

The letters from the apostle Paul to Timothy and Titus are known as the Pastoral Epistles. Paul wrote these letters to give these two young pastors instructions regarding doctrine, administration, and false teachers. These letters also reveal a very personal side of the apostle. Paul knew the days of his martyrdom were approaching so he took the opportunity to shepherd the hearts and minds of the next generation of church leaders. In this lecture, Dr. Sproul discusses the Pastoral Epistles.

SCRIPTURE READING

1 and 2 Thessalonians, 1 and 2 Timothy, Titus

LEARNING OBJECTIVES

1. To identify the purpose of the Pastoral Epistles.

2. To discuss the qualifications Paul outlines for church leaders.

3. To identify the significance of the Apostolic Tradition.

QUOTATIONS

The Pastorals provide insight for dealing with contemporary problems of heresy, divisiveness, and leadership difficulties. They are not a collection of rigid rules for church organization, but they are guidelines providing direction for facing problems and church needs.

The Pastorals are realistic. They present the churches Paul founded with all their needs, weaknesses, and shortcomings. However, they also present the mighty power of God as a prescription to human failure, and they show this divine power at work in the lives of people.

The Pastorals provide encouragement. Despite the likelihood that Paul was facing death as he wrote 2 Timothy, he remained steadfastly optimistic. He was lonely, but he was vigilant, irrepressibly a preacher, and confident in the Lord. The Pastorals provide a picture of the early church as it faced error, greed, and moral turpitude. Despite these shortcomings there is a clear sign of anticipated victory and hopeful moral restitution. churches today need a heavy dose of such realism and encouragement.

—Thomas D. Lea and Hayne P. Griffin

LECTURE OUTLINE

A. The epistles of 1 and 2 Timothy and Titus are known as the Pastoral Epistles.
   - Paul gives instructions regarding the ordering and administering of the local church in these letters.

B. Paul traveled throughout the Roman Empire establishing churches and appointing believers to leadership.
   1. Timothy was probably appointed to leadership over the church in Ephesus after Paul's departure.

   2. Timothy was mentored as Paul's apprentice.

   3. Second Timothy is a very personal letter to Timothy as Paul approaches the end of his life.

   4. Paul emphasized the importance of pure doctrine to Timothy and urged him to guard against the false teachers infecting his congregation.

   5. Paul saw no artificial division between pure doctrine and practice.

C. "This saying is trustworthy. If anyone aspires to the office of overseer, he desires a noble task. Therefore an overseer must be above reproach, the husband of one wife, sober-minded, self-controlled, respectable, hospitable, able to teach, not a drunkard, not violent but gentle, not quarrelsome, not a lover of money. He must manage his own household well, with all dignity keeping his children submissive, for if someone does not know how to manage his own household, how will he care for God's church? He must not be recent convert, or he may become puffed up with conceit and fall into the condemnation of the devil. Moreover, he must be well thought of by outsiders, so that he may not fall into disgrace, into a snare of the devil" (1 Tim. 3:1–7).
   1. The qualifications Paul outlines for church leadership seem unattainable.

   2. Paul is most likely using a literary device here called a *panegyric*.

3. A *panegyric* is a public oration celebrating the life of a well known person.

4. Nobody in a congregation demonstrates these qualities without fail, but they are the qualities to which an elder or deacon should aspire.

5. The church has long debated the meaning of Paul's requirement that an elder be the husband of one wife.

6. Some have interpreted the statement as a prohibition against one who is divorced or a widower who remarries.

7. Probably the best interpretation is that Paul is placing a requirement of monogamy on the elders and deacons of a church.

D. "Deacons likewise must be dignified, not double-tongued, not addicted to much wine, not greedy for dishonest gain. They must hold the mystery of the faith with a clear conscience. And let them also be tested first; then let them serve as deacons if they prove themselves blameless. Their wives likewise must be dignified, not slanderers, but sober-minded, faithful in all things" (1 Tim. 3:8–11).
    •   Those who desire to be leaders in the church must aspire to these character qualities.

E. Paul wrote 2 Timothy near the end of his life.
    1. Timothy was a young disciple of Paul who replaced John Mark.

    2. Timothy continued with Paul on his missionary journeys and John Mark wrote the gospel of Mark.

    3. Paul wrote 2 Timothy as his final instructions to continue his work after his death.

F. "But understand this, that in the last days there will come times of difficulty. For people will be lovers of self, lovers of money, proud, arrogant, abusive, disobedient to their parents, ungrateful, unholy, heartless, unappeasable, slanderous, without self-control, brutal, not loving good, treacherous, reckless, swollen with conceit, lovers of pleasure rather than lovers of God, having the appearance of godliness, but denying its power. Avoid such people" (2 Tim. 3:1–5).
    1. Paul predicts that the church will backslide into false teaching and immorality.

    2. The church will have the outward appearance of religion, but lack a core of truth and substance.

G. "You, however, have followed my teaching, my conduct, my aim in life, my faith, my
    patience, my love, my steadfastness, my persecutions and sufferings that happened
    to me at Antioch, at Iconium, and at Lystra—which persecutions I endured; yet from
    them all the Lord rescued me. Indeed, all who desire to live a godly life in Christ Jesus
    will be persecuted, while evil people and impostors will go on from bad to worse,
    deceiving and being deceived. But as for you, continue in what you have learned and
    have firmly believed, knowing from who you learned it" (2 Tim. 3:10–14).
    1. Paul encourages Timothy to preserve the Apostolic Tradition which was a
        body of knowledge and practice handed down by the apostles to succeeding
        generations.

    2. Ancient Israel was likewise commanded to teach each new generation the
        law and the great things God had done in the nation's past.

H. "All Scripture is breathed out by God and profitable for teaching, for reproof, for
    correction, and for training in righteousness, that the man of God may be compe-
    tent, equipped for every good work" (2 Tim. 3:16–17).
    1. This is an important text for the self-testimony of the Bible.

    2. The Bible authenticates itself as the very Word of God and requires the vali-
        dation of no man to be true.

    3. The origin of all Scripture is from the mind of God and not man.

I. "I charge you in the presence of God and of Christ Jesus, who is to judge the living
    and the dead, and by his appearing and his kingdom: preach the Word; be ready in
    season and out of season; reprove, rebuke, and exhort, with complete patience and
    teaching. For the time is coming when people will not endure sound teaching, but
    having itching ears they will accumulate for themselves teachers to suit their own
    passions, and will turn away from listening to the truth and wander off into myths.
    As for you, always be sober-minded, endure suffering, do the work of an evangelist,
    fulfill your ministry" (2 Tim. 4:1–5).
    1. Paul's apostolic charge to Timothy is to preach the Word with faithfulness,
        courage, perseverance, and patience despite the suffering that will come.

    2. The false prophets are those who preach to the itching ears of their listeners
        and proclaim only what the people want to hear.

J. "For I am already being poured out as a drink offering, and the time of my departure
    has come. I have fought the good fight, I have finished the race, I have kept the faith.
    Henceforth there is laid for me the crown of righteousness, which the Lord, the
    righteous judge, will award to me on that day, and not only to me but also to all who
    have loved his appearing" (2 Tim. 4:6–8).

1. Paul was most likely beheaded during the reign of Emperor Nero shortly after writing these words.

2. Paul poured out his life and made himself a living sacrifice for the praise Christ and the benefit of others.

BIBLE STUDY

1. What do you think the Thessalonians were worried about regarding those who had died in Christ? How does Paul comfort and instruct them in 1 Thessalonians 3:13ff.?

2. What encouragement does Paul offer the Thessalonians amidst their persecution in 2 Thessalonians 1:3–12?

3. How were the false teachers abusing the law of Moses in Timothy's church? What does Paul mean by saying that the law is not for the just or righteous in 1 Timothy 1:9? What do the just have if not the law according to verse 11?

4. What instructions does Paul give to men and women regarding worship in 1 Timothy 2:8–15? How can we apply his instructions to the modern church?

5. The letters to Timothy and Titus are commonly designated the "Pastoral Epistles" because they are addressed to individuals with pastoral duties. Titus was one of these individuals. In Titus 1:6–9 Paul outlines the qualifications for elders. What are an elder's personal and family life to be? What are the sins and vices from which an elder must be free? What are the virtues he must possess?

DISCUSSION

1. What does Paul teach Timothy about money in 1 Timothy (see chap. 6, for example)? What do you think were the false ideas about money being circulated in Timothy's church?

2. What are Paul's concerns as he approaches his death according to 2 Timothy 3–4? What does this reveal about the Apostle to the Gentiles?

3. Read Titus 1:16 and compare it to Titus 1:1. Can we consider a person a believer who claims to believe but who is continually disobedient to the commands of God? Why or why not? How does it affect the assurance of your salvation when you are in sin (Ps. 51)?

FOR FURTHER STUDY

Guthrie, Donald. *The Pastoral Epistles*
Knight, George W., III. *The Pastoral Epistles*

53

Hebrews

MESSAGE INTRODUCTION

No other book in the New Testament integrates the gospel with the Old Testament better than the book of Hebrews. The unknown writer of this epistle is relentless in his effort to reveal Christ as greater than the prophets, angels, Moses, and the Levitical priests. In fact all the ceremonies, sacrifices, and offices of the Old Testament foreshadow the person and work of Jesus Christ. In light of so great a salvation, the Hebrews are encouraged to run the race before them in faithfulness and perseverance. In this lecture, Dr. Sproul discusses the book of Hebrews.

SCRIPTURE READING

Hebrews

LEARNING OBJECTIVES

1. To discuss the debate surrounding the authorship of Hebrews.

2. To identify Christ's order of priesthood.

3. To explain the role of the lapsi in early church history.

QUOTATIONS

There is, indeed, no book in the Holy Scriptures which speaks so clearly of the priesthood of Christ, so highly exalts the virtue and dignity of that only true sacrifice which he offered by his death, so abundantly treats of the use of ceremonies as well as of their abrogation, and, in a word, so fully explains that Christ is the end of the Law.

—John Calvin

LECTURE OUTLINE

A. Hebrews integrates the world of the Old Testament with that of the New Testament.
   - The excellence and preeminence of Christ is emphasized throughout the book of Hebrews.

B. "Long ago, at many times and in many ways, God spoke to our fathers by the prophets, but in these last days he has spoken to us by his Son, whom he appointed the heir of all things, through whom also he created the world. He is the radiance of the glory of God and the exact imprint of his nature, and he upholds the universe by the word of his power. After making purification for sins, he sat down at the right hand of the Majesty on high, having become as much superior to angels as the name he has inherited is more excellent than theirs" (Heb. 1:1–4).
   1. Many consider Hebrews to be an extended sermon or homily on the superior excellence of Christ.

   2. Hebrews demonstrates some of the highest literary quality in the New Testament.

C. The early church debated extensively whether or not Hebrews belonged in the canon of Scripture.
   1. Early church leaders included Hebrews in the canon of Scripture believing it was written by the apostle Paul.

   2. Modern Bible scholars do not believe Paul wrote Hebrews because of the literary differences between Hebrews and the Pauline epistles.

   3. The authorship of Hebrews is widely debated yet unresolved.

D. It is also unknown to whom the book was written and amidst what circumstances.

E. Some have argued the purpose of Hebrews was to counter the Judaizers or the Gnostics.
   - Others have suggested the purpose was to inspire perseverance amidst persecution.

F. Hebrews may have been written to address the problem of the first century lapsi.
   1. The *lapsi* were the Christians who renounced their faith upon persecution and who were not faithful unto death.

   2. Hebrews may have been written for this group to encourage them to persevere and remain faithful to Christ even unto death.

G. Hebrews describes Christ as the greatest revelation of God and the brightness of the glory of God.

   1. The majesty of the invisible God was revealed in the wilderness by the shekinah cloud that hovered over the Tabernacle.

   2. The brightness of God's glory outshines the sun.

   3. The Son of God is the brightness of the glory of God and the exact image of His person.

   4. The greatest manifestation of the invisible God was the incarnation of Jesus Christ.

H. Christ is described as greater than the angels in order to counter the Gnostic heresy that made Christ out to be nothing more than an angelic being.

   • Christ is the creator and lord of the angels.

I. Christ is compared with the old covenant and its mediator Moses.

   • Moses was a faithful servant in God's house, but Christ is the lord of the house.

J. Hebrews discusses the superiority of Christ's priesthood.

   1. Old Testament sacrifices needed to be repeated continuously.

   2. Old Testament sacrifices and rituals were signs of better realities to come.

   3. The best and real sacrifice was made by Christ one time and does not need to be repeated.

K. Priests were required to be Levites in the Old Testament.

   1. Jesus was born into the line of Judah.

   2. Jesus' priesthood is from the order of Melchizedek.

   3. The priesthood of Melchizedek is described as greater than the priesthood of the Levites.

L. Jesus is shown to be superior to the prophets, angels, Moses, and the Levitical priesthood in the book of Hebrews.

M. The writer of Hebrews urges his readers to move on from the elementary teachings of the faith and grow into maturity.

- The Hebrews are encouraged to persevere and remain faithful amidst persecution and false teaching.

N. The Hebrews are reminded of the rebellion of the Israelites in the wilderness.
    1. Their disbelief caused them to fail to enter God's rest.

    2. None can escape God's judgment if they neglect "so great a salvation" as we have in Christ.

O. All religions are not equal and salvation is only to be found in faith in Jesus Christ.

P. Hebrews 11 celebrates those in the Old Testament who persevered and lived by faith.

Q. The Hebrews are encouraged to persevere in faith until the end.

BIBLE STUDY

1. What is God's greatest means of speaking to His children in the latter days according to Hebrews 1:1–3? What honors has God given Jesus that make Him greater than the angels according to Hebrews 1?

2. Why does Jesus qualify to raise believers up as His brothers and sisters (Heb. 2, 5)? How did He become like us? How do we become like Him?

3. What was the rest promised to the people of God in the wilderness (Heb. 3–4)? Why did they fail to receive it? What is the new place of rest promised to the people of God? How is it possible for us to fail to receive it?

4. How is the priesthood of Melchizedek superior to that of the Levites (Heb. 7)? Why is it significant that Jesus comes from this line of priests?

5. How is the new covenant superior to the old covenant in the following areas: priesthood, sacrifice, intercession, sanctuary, promises, forgiveness?

6. What privilege have we been granted through the blood of Jesus (Heb. 10:19–22)? How should we live in response to this privilege?

DISCUSSION

1. Why is the spiritual growth of the Hebrews stalled according to chapter 6? What is the writer's desire for the spiritually sluggish Hebrews? How might this speak to our lives today?

2. What role does the faith chapter of Hebrews 11 play in the writer's argument? After reading the book of Hebrews, who can we conclude are those who receive God's approval?

3. How does the author of Hebrews contrast two mountains in Hebrews 12:18–24? What is the significance of this contrast for believers?

FOR FURTHER STUDY

Lane, William. *Hebrews*
Owen, John. *An Exposition of the Epistle to the Hebrews*

54

General Epistles

MESSAGE INTRODUCTION

Hebrews, James, 1 and 2 Peter, 1–3 John, and Jude are known as the General Epistles. These letters were most likely written to circulate among several congregations and not a specific church. It is difficult to determine the audience for whom some of these letters were originally written, but each of these books are relevant for the modern church. The author of Hebrew's celebration of Christ, Peter and Jude's call to faithfulness, and John's call to love one another are messages that still need to be heard by the church today. In this lecture, Dr. Sproul discusses the General Epistles.

SCRIPTURE READING

James, 1–2 Peter, 1–3 John, Jude

LEARNING OBJECTIVES

1. To discuss the book of James as an example of New Testament wisdom literature.

2. To explain the role of suffering in the epistles of Peter.

3. To identify the heresy John refutes in his epistles.

QUOTATIONS

Such evidence as survives from the last four decades of the first century reveals that the churches were "by heresies distressed" as well as "by schisms rent asunder." Digressions from truth occurred in every direction and constant vigilance was necessary if the Christians were to keep their faith pure.

Five short epistles, 2 Peter, Jude, 1, 2, and 3 John, were written to cope with these trends toward false doctrines within the church. Controversy was not their sole aim, nor was their subject matter devoted entirely to attacking heresy. Their approach was positive rather than negative, as their outlines will show. They were, however, all colored by the dangers of the times, in which the church was threatened quite as much by the subtle infiltration of paganism into its thinking as by the frontal attacks of persecution from without.

—Merrill C. Tenney

LECTURE OUTLINE

A. Hebrews, James, 1 and 2 Peter, 1–3 John, and Jude are known as the General Epistles.
  - These letters were written most likely to circulate among several congregations and were not written to a specific church.

B. The book of James is considered to be the only New Testament example of wisdom literature.
  1. James exudes a style that hearkens back to Jewish wisdom literature.

  2. The author of the book of James was probably also the brother of Jesus.

  3. James presided over the Council of Jerusalem in Acts 15.

  4. He apparently did not believe in the messianic mission of Jesus originally, but later became a leader in the Jerusalem church and was known as James the Just.

C. The book of James cites aphorisms that reflect the teaching of Jesus more frequently than any other New Testament epistle.
  - It is possible that James records some of Jesus' teaching that was not recorded in the Gospels.

D. "James, a servant of God and of the Lord Jesus Christ, to the twelve tribes in the Dispersion: Greetings. Count it all joy, my brothers, when you meet trials of various kinds, for you know that the testing of your faith produces steadfastness. And let steadfastness have its full effect, that you may be perfect and complete, lacking in nothing. If any of you lacks wisdom, let him ask God, who gives generously to all without reproach, and it will be given him. But let him ask in faith, with no doubting, for the one who doubts is like a wave of the sea that is driven and tossed by the wind. For that person must not suppose that he will receive anything from the Lord; he is a double-minded man, unstable in all his ways" (James 1:1–8).

1. The purpose of our struggles is sanctification and our posture towards our struggles is wisdom.

2. Jewish wisdom emphasized practical advice on how to live a godly life.

E. James emphasizes the role of works as the natural expression of our faith.
    1. Believers enjoy a royal liberty to obey Christ as they are not under the law.

    2. The freedom of the Christian is not a license to sin, but rather a freedom to walk in the Spirit in obedience to Christ.

F. James particularly warns against the perils of an ungoverned tongue.
    1. The tongue is like the rudder of a great ship which as a small component it can steer the entire vessel.

    2. The tongue is also compared to a spark that ignites a forest and an animal that cannot be tamed.

G. James encourages his readers to remember that the continual prayers of the righteous do not go unheeded by the Lord.
    • He closes his epistle reminding his readers that believers must be people of their word.

H. Peter encourages his readers to remain faithful amidst persecution in his two epistles.
    1. The health-and-wealth gospel is a betrayal of the truths of Scripture.

    2. Believing in Jesus does not guarantee immediate prosperity and health.

    3. The question for the believer is not *if* they will suffer, but rather *when* will they suffer for the sake of the kingdom.

I. "Blessed be the God and Father of our Lord Jesus Christ! According to his great mercy, he has caused us to be born again to a living hope through the resurrection of Jesus Christ from the dead, to an inheritance that is imperishable, undefiled, and unfading, kept in heaven for you, who by God's power are being guarded through faith for a salvation ready to be revealed in the last time" (1 Peter 1:3–5).
    1. God has given us a new birth that comes with a heavenly inheritance that is incorruptible, undefiled, and guaranteed.

    2. Believers rejoice in a heavenly treasure, promise, and inheritance rather than an earthly reward.

3. "In this you rejoice, though now for a little while, if necessary, you have been grieved by various trials, so that the tested genuineness of your faith—more precious than gold that perishes though it is tested by fire—may be found to result in praise and glory and honor at the revelation of Jesus Christ. Though you have not seen him, you love him. Though you do not now see him, you believe in him and rejoice with joy that is inexpressible and filled with glory, obtaining the outcome of your faith, the salvation of your souls" (1 Peter 1:6–9).

1. The purpose of our sufferings is not to destroy us, but rather to refine our souls.

2. God is using our pain for our purification and sanctification.

J. "Beloved, do not be surprised at the fiery trial when it comes upon you to test you, as though something strange were happening to you. But rejoice insofar as you share Christ's sufferings, that you may also rejoice and be glad when his glory is revealed. If you are insulted for the name of Christ, you are blessed, because the Spirit of glory and of God rests upon you" (1 Peter 4:12–14).
   • God is not punishing us when we endure affliction, but rather promises His presence amidst our tribulations.

K. A primary theme in the epistles of John is loving one another within the body of Christ.

L. John is also concerned like Peter about the invasion of heresy into the church.
   • He warns the church against the spirit of the antichrist that is already working within the world.

M. John is writing against the heresy of Docetism which as an offshoot of Gnosticism denied the human nature of Christ.
   1. Some of the Greeks believed matter and human nature were evil and that God would never take on human flesh.

   2. It is important that Christians affirm the deity and the humanity of Christ as Savior.

BIBLE STUDY

1. Why is it important to James to emphasize good works in 2:14–26? How can we reconcile these verses with Paul's words in Galatians 3:10–14 and Romans 3:21–22?

2. Many have identified the book of James with the genre of "wisdom literature" found in the Proverbs and Ecclesiastes, making it very proverbial in its application. Others have claimed that this book is formal doctrinal teaching, like Ephesians or Romans, making its application very straightforward. How do these two views affect the meaning of James 3:1 and the rest of the chapter as it focuses on the tongue and the heart it reveals?

3. In 1 Peter 1:3–4, Peter tells us something about our hope. Why do believers have hope? What kind of inheritance do believers have? In verses 5–9 he address the problem of enduring through trials. Why are believers able to greatly rejoice even in the midst of trials and suffering?

4. What were the false teachers saying about the second coming of Christ according to 2 Peter 3? Why does Peter discuss the Flood in this passage? What is God waiting for before the Last Judgment?

5. Read 1 John 1:1–4. Why do you suppose it was important for John to open his letter in this manner, discussing as he does, the fact that the "Word of life" was not merely seen or heard but "touched with hands"?

DISCUSSION

1. How does Peter describe the identity of Christ and believers using temple imagery in 1 Peter 2:4–12? What responsibilities come with the identity believers have been given? Similarly, what does it mean in 2 Peter 1:4 to share God's promises and His divine nature? How should remembering our inheritance impact our daily living?

2. In 1 John 1:9, the author says in effect that if we confess our sins to God, He, being faithful and consistent, will do what is right (just), He will "forgive us our sins and cleanse us from all unrighteousness." Why do you think that this is "right" for God to do? What do you think God is being faithful to when He does forgive sins?

3. Why can believers rejoice in the destruction of the wicked that Jude describes? What role do the wicked play in God's plan of redemption?

FOR FURTHER STUDY

Kruse, Colin G. *The Letters of John*
Moo, Douglas J. *2 Peter, Jude*
_____. *The Letter of James*

55

Introduction to Revelation

MESSAGE INTRODUCTION

Eschatology is the study of the "last things" or end times. It is one of the most exciting, but also one of the most difficult fields of theological study. The book of Revelation is one of the most important resources we have for understanding eschatology. Even though its symbols, characters, and events can be difficult to understand, its pages contain God's encouragement for His people during times of persecution and trial. In this lecture, Dr. Sproul introduces the book of Revelation.

SCRIPTURE READING

Revelation 1–3

LEARNING OBJECTIVES

1. To show the significance of eschatology and apocalyptic literature for God's people.

2. To identify four common approaches to the book of Revelation.

3. To examine the evidence available for dating the book of Revelation.

QUOTATIONS

In some ways, Revelation is the outworking of what Jesus told Peter, "On this rock I will build my church, and the gates of hell shall not prevail against it" (Matt. 16:18). If these words from Matthew comprise the still photograph, the Book of Revelation is the movie. In a day when the visual and cinematic take precedence over the written word, the genre of Revelation seems particularly suitable.

Revelation is a book of pictures designed to appeal to the visual senses. As we turn over its pages, we are meant to be overwhelmed by its descriptions of the Savior. Noting, that the prevailing command in the book is not "Listen!" but "Look!" we are being introduced to the idea that Revelation is about pictures as well as about words.

—Derek Thomas

LECTURE OUTLINE

A. *Eschatology* is the study of the "last things" or end times.
    1. Eschatology includes study of the *parousia* or "appearing" of Christ, the rapture, resurrection, the antichrist, heaven, and hell.

    2. The *eschaton* is the last age highlighted by the consummation of the kingdom of God.

    3. It is difficult to establish a scholarly consensus regarding prophecies of the end times.

B. Eschatological prophecies are presented in Scripture in many figures and symbols known as apocalyptic literature.
    1. The book of Revelation is also known as the apocalypse.

    2. *Apocalypse* means "revealing" or "unveiling".

    3. Some scholars have argued apocalyptic literature was written in code during times of persecution in order to secretly communicate.

C. The best method for interpreting the symbols and signs of apocalyptic literature is to interpret them in light of the rest of Scripture.

D. There are many schools of thought for interpreting the Apocalypse including premillennialism, postmillennialism, amillennialism, post-tribulationism, midtribulationism, and pre-tribulationism.

E. There are four primary approaches to the book of Revelation.
    1. *The Preterist* view argues the prophecies of the book focus primarily on events of the first century and particularly the destruction of Jerusalem in 70 AD.

    2. *The Futurist* view argues the prophecies of the book will be fulfilled near the second coming of Christ and therefore have not yet occurred.

    3. *The Historicist* view argues the prophecies of the book are chronologically being fulfilled over the course of church history and will be climaxed with the return of Christ.

    4. *The Idealist* view argues the prophecies are symbols of the ongoing struggle between God and Satan throughout church history.

F. The interpretive approach one adopts for reading the book of Revelation will affect one's understanding of the book.

G. Evangelical scholars generally agree that the book of Revelation was written by the apostle John.
- John was the last of Jesus' original twelve disciples and the only one to die a natural death.

H. Establishing the date of composition for the book of Revelation is a very significant question that will affect an interpretation of the book.

I. The traditional date of the book of Revelation was the late 90s AD.
    1. Some modern scholars have argued the book was written in the 60s AD.

    2. Dating the book of Revelation before or after the fall of Jerusalem in 70 AD has a significant impact on an interpretation of the book.

J. There are two types of evidence scholars examine in order to date a piece of writing.
    1. External evidence examines information outside of the document for establishing a composition date.

    2. Internal evidence examines the information provided by the document itself for establishing a composition date.

K. There is significant external evidence that helps scholars date the book of Revelation.
- Ireneus dated the book during the reign of Domitian who ruled in the last decade of the first century.

L. The book of Revelation also provides internal evidence that helps scholars establish a composition date for the book.
- There are many chronological references in the book of Revelation.

M. "The revelation of Jesus Christ, which God gave him to show to his servants the things that must soon take place. He made it known by sending his angel to his servant John, who bore witness to the Word of God and to the testimony of Jesus Christ, even to all that he saw. Blessed is the one who reads aloud the words of this prophecy, and blessed are those who hear, and who keep what is written in it, for the time is near" (Rev. 1:1–3).

1. Two time references are included in this passage.

2. John is recording events that are near and will soon come to pass.

3. Various scholars have interpreted these words in a very strict or loose manner.

4. The relationship between the destruction of the temple and the composition of Revelation is difficult to resolve.

N. "This calls for a mind with wisdom: the seven heads are seven mountains on which the woman is seated; they are also seven kings, five of whom have fallen, one is, the other has not yet come, and when he does come he must remain only a little while. As for the beast that was and is not, it is an eighth but it belongs to the seven, and it goes to destruction" (Rev. 17:9–11).
   - Some interpreters believe this passage forecasts the rise and fall of Emperor Nero and his persecution against the church.

O. The book of Revelation has been a source of encouragement for the people of God during periods of persecution throughout the ages.

BIBLE STUDY

1. Who are the individuals involved in transmitting the book of Revelation according to Revelation 1:1–2? To what audience was this writing originally directed?

2. What is the promise and the warning Revelation gives regarding itself in Revelation 1:3 and 22:18–19? How does this affect our doctrine of Scripture (what parameters does it provide)?

3. John describes Jesus as the "ruler of the kings of the earth" in Revelation 1:5, and the Father is described as "Alpha and Omega Who is, and Who was, and Who is to come" in 1:8. How may these descriptions have been interpreted by the original audience who were enduring political persecution for their faith? How might these descriptions of God influence your perception of suffering?

4. How does John describe each member of the Trinity in Revelation 1:4–8? Since seven is commonly thought to be a symbolic number in Semitic culture indicating perfection, why might John have described the Holy Spirit as "seven spirits" or the "sevenfold Spirit"?

5. Reading through all seven letters found in Revelation, how does Christ Jesus commend and rebuke each of the churches mentioned therein?

DISCUSSION

1. How does Jesus' self-identification in Revelation 1:17 compare to the Father's identification in Revelation 1:8? How are they different and similar? Also compare this to Jesus' self designation in Revelation 22:12–13. What does this indicate about the identity of the Father and the Son?

2. What are the promises Christ gives to those who overcome in each of the churches? How are the promises simultaneously a present reality and a future expectation?

3. In Revelation 5:10, what roles do those who are purchased by the blood of the Lamb fill? How might this give meaning to your Christian identity and service?

FOR FURTHER STUDY

Beale, G.K. *The Book of Revelation*
Johnson, Dennis E. *Triumph of the Lamb*
Pate, C. Marvin. *Four Views on the Book of Revelation*

56

The Christ of Revelation

MESSAGE INTRODUCTION

The triumph of Jesus Christ and His kingdom is the story of all of Scripture. Nowhere is this message as clear as in the book of Revelation. John describes Christ as the victor over the grave in chapter one, the vengeful harvester in chapter fourteen, and the divine conqueror in chapter nineteen. Yet perhaps John's most surprising image of Christ occurs in chapter five where the Savior is depicted as a slain lamb. Only the Lamb of God who takes away the sin of the world is worthy to open God's scroll of judgment against the wicked. In this lecture, Dr. Sproul discusses the Christ of Revelation.

SCRIPTURE READING

Revelation 4–11

LEARNING OBJECTIVES

1. To identify the Old Testament background of the book of Revelation.

2. To explain John's vision of heaven in Revelation chapter five.

3. To highlight the theme of Christ's victory in Revelation.

QUOTATIONS

The purpose of the Apocalypse is to encourage and comfort believers in their struggle against Satan and his cohorts. The book divulges that in this conflict between Christ and Satan, Christ is the victor and Satan the vanquished. Even though Satan and his army wage war against the saints on earth, who endure suffering, oppression, persecution, and death, Christ is victorious. It is Christ who encourages his people to withstand the onslaughts of the evil one, for they too will reign with Christ and will be seated with him on his throne. Jesus extends comfort to all believers, for God sees their tears and wipes them away. God listens to their prayers and in response he will influence the course of history. Saints who die in the Lord are called blessed, for their good deeds are not forgotten. The blood of martyrs will be avenged; saints clothed in white apparel are present at the wedding of the Lamb; and they will reign with Christ forever.

—Simon Kistemaker

LECTURE OUTLINE

A. The book of Revelation is full of allusions and references to the Old Testament.

B. A proper understanding of Scripture incorporates both Testaments and sees the New Testament as a fulfillment of the Old Testament.

C. The triumph of Christ and His kingdom is a central powerful theme in the book of Revelation.

D. "After this I looked, and behold, a door standing open in heaven! And the first voice, which I had heard speaking to me like a trumpet, said, 'Come up here, and I will show you what must take place after this.' At once I was in the Spirit, and behold, a throne stood in heaven, with one seated on the throne. And he who sat there had the appearance of jasper and carnelian, and around the throne was a rainbow that had the appearance of an emerald. Around the throne were twenty-four thrones, and seated on the thrones were twenty-four elders, clothed in white garments, with golden crowns on their heads. From the throne came flashes of lightning, and rumblings and peals of thunder, and before the throne were burning seven torches of fire, which are the seven spirits of God, and before the throne there was as it were a sea of glass, like crystal. And around the throne, on each side of the throne, are four living creatures, full of eyes in front and behind: the first living creature like a lion, the second living creature like an ox, the third living creature with the face of a man, and the fourth living creature like an eagle in flight. And the four living creatures, each of them with six wings, are full of eyes all around and within, and day and night they never cease to say, 'Holy, holy, holy, is the Lord God Almighty, who was and is and is to come!'" (Rev. 4:1–8).

1. John uses imagery very common in the Old Testament.

2. John's vision is very similar to Ezekiel's vision of God's chariot throne in Ezekiel 1.

3. The words of the four living creatures is very similar to the words of the seraphim in Isaiah's vision in Isaiah 6.

E.   "And whenever the living creatures give glory and honor and thanks to him who is seated on the throne, who lives forever and ever, the twenty-four elders fall down before him who is seated on the throne and worship him who lives forever and ever. They cast their crowns before the throne, saying, 'Worthy are you, our Lord and God, to receive glory and honor and power, for you created all things, and by your will they existed and were created'" (Rev. 4: 9–11).

F.   John is given a vision of the inner chamber of the heavenly sanctuary in Revelation 4 and 5.

G.   "Then I saw in the right hand of him who was seated on the throne a scroll written within and on the back, sealed with seven seals" (Rev. 5:1).

1.   Most texts in the classical world were written on one side of a scroll.

2.   Ezekiel was commanded to eat a scroll of judgment written on both sides (Ez. 2:8–10).

3.   The double sided scroll John sees in Revelation 5 is also probably a scroll of judgment written against the wicked.

H.   "And I saw a strong angel proclaiming with a loud voice, 'Who is worthy to open the scroll and break its seals?'" (Rev. 5:2).

1.   Some commentators have argued the book of Revelation was written as a drama with acts and scenes.

2.   The drama of one worthy to open the seals on the scroll opens up the rest of the book of Revelation.

I.   "And no one in heaven or on earth or under the earth was able to open the scroll or to look into it, and I began to weep loudly because no one was found worthy to open the scroll or to look into it" (Rev. 5:4).

•   The suspense of events builds without anyone worthy to open the scroll.

J.   "And one of the elders said to me, 'Weep no more; behold, the Lion of the tribe of Judah, the Root of David, has conquered, so that he can open the scroll and its seven seals'" (Rev. 5:5).

•   The elder refers John back to the Old Testament because the promise of royalty was given to the tribe of Judah.

K. "And between the throne and the four living creatures and among the elders I saw a Lamb standing, as though it had been slain, with seven horns and with seven eyes, which are the seven spirits of God sent out into all the earth. And he went and took the scroll from the right hand of him who was seated on the throne. And when he had taken the scroll, the four living creatures and the twenty-four elders fell down before the Lamb, each holding a harp, and golden bowls full of incense, which are the prayers of the saints. And they sang a new song," (Rev. 5:6–9a).

1. John is expecting to see a powerful lion, but instead he sees a lamb that had been slaughtered.

2. A new song of worship is sung to celebrate a new work of redemption.

3. The Lamb is worshipped because He alone is worthy to open the scroll.

L. "And they sang a new song, saying, 'Worthy are you to take the scroll and to open its seals, for you were slain, and by your blood from every tribe and language and people and nation, and you have made them a kingdom and priests to our God, and they shall reign on the earth.' Then I looked, and I heard around the throne and the living creatures and the elders the voice of many angels, numbering myriads of myriads and thousands of thousands, saying with a loud voice, 'Worthy is the Lamb who was slain, to receive power and wealth and wisdom and might and honor and glory and blessing!' And I heard every creature in heaven and on earth and under the earth and in the sea, and all that is in them, saying, 'To him who sits on the throne and to the Lamb be blessing and honor and glory and might forever and ever!' And the four living creatures said, 'Amen!' and the elders fell down and worshiped" (Rev. 5:9–14).

1. Regardless of the method one adopts to interpret the book of Revelation it clear the Lamb has won the greatest victory.

2. The Lamb owns the book of life that contains the names of those whose futures are sealed in Him.

BIBLE STUDY

1. Chapters 4 and 5 are a prefix to the terrible judgment oracles that follow in the book of Revelation. It is as if God wants to assure John's audience that things are in order in heaven, regardless of the apparent state of things on the earth. How might 4:2 assist such believers as they endured the judgment of worldly rulers?

2. Notice the anthem of praise in Revelation 4:11. What is the activity of God that is extolled in these verses? According to John 1:3 and Colossians 1:16–17, what person of the Godhead did the Father use to do this work?

3. Contrast the fate of the righteous with the fate of those on the earth in Revelation 6 and 7? What are the symbols John uses to communicate this contrast?

4. Why is the image of the saints washing their robes in the blood of the Lamb an appropriate description of conversion (Rev. 7:14)? What are the blessings the saints enjoy as a result of this washing (vv. 15–17)?

5. How are the two witnesses of Revelation 11 an appropriate symbol of the witnessing church throughout the ages? How does John forecast the ultimate victory of the church?

6. How does the theme of "now, but not yet" frequently get played out in Revelation regarding the triumph of Christ, the victory of the saints, the defeat of Satan, and the establishment of God's kingdom?

DISCUSSION

1. Imagine that you are observing the scene in Revelation 5:11–14. How might your attitude toward worship change if you knew this assembly joined with you each time you lifted up praises to the Lord? Though we can hardly believe it, who does Hebrews 12:22–24 indicate that we participate with as we worship? How might this affect the way you participate in private and corporate worship?

2. What does John mean in Revelation 11:15 when he writes that the kingdom of the world has become the kingdom of the Lord? How will the triumph of the kingdom impact (anticipated first in the church's life) politics, economics, art, families, culture, and technology?

3. The first eleven chapters of Revelation detail the world's persecution against the church. The last eleven chapters of Revelation reveal the final conflict between Christ and Satan. Why do you think the book is structured this way?

FOR FURTHER STUDY

Bauckham, Richard. *The Theology of the Book of Revelation*
Beale, G.K. *The Book of Revelation*
Johnson, Dennis E. *Triumph of the Lamb*
Mathison, Keith A. *From Age to Age*

57

The Glory of God

MESSAGE INTRODUCTION

Death is the common enemy of all mankind. Man was created from the dust and can only anticipate death and a return to the dust apart from divine intervention. The resurrection of Jesus offers believers a new hope. Rather than being created from the dust and returning to the dust, Christians can joyfully look forward to conquering the grave and rising to glory. Only those who participate in the death and resurrection of Jesus Christ can look forward to an eternal citizenship in the glorious New Jerusalem. In this lecture, Dr. Sproul discusses the glory of God.

SCRIPTURE READING

Revelation 12–22

LEARNING OBJECTIVES

1. To identify the hope of glory that believers in Christ share.

2. To examine the promises of glory detailed in the book of Revelation.

3. To define the relationship between God and His people in the New Jerusalem.

QUOTATIONS

For behold, the winter is past
the rain is over and gone.
The flowers appear on the earth,
the time of singing has come.
—Song of Songs 2:11–12

O Lᴏʀᴅ, our Lᴏʀᴅ, how majestic is your name in all the earth! You have set your glory above the heavens . . . When I look at your heavens, the work of your fingers, the moon and the stars, which you have set in place, what is man that you are mindful of him, and the son of man that you care for him?

—Psalm 8:1, 3–4

LECTURE OUTLINE

A. "Dust to dust and ashes to ashes" is a common recitation at funerals.
   1. The life of the redeemed endures beyond the dust and moves from dust to glory.

   2. The perspective of the New Testament is that believers enter a far greater existence and glory upon death and do not simply return to the dust from which they were created.

   3. We need to keep the destiny and hope of our faith in front of us lest we become attached to the passing things of this world.

B. "Then I saw a new heaven and a new earth, for the first heaven and the first earth had passed away, and the sea was no more" (Rev. 21:1).
   1. The sea in Hebrew literature was traditionally the image of conflict and chaos.

   2. The Hebrews had not developed a coastal trade because of a rocky coastline and because they were barraged by strong winds and marauders from the sea.

   3. Rivers, streams, and springs are images of life and blessedness in Hebrew literature.

   4. The absence of the sea in the new heavens and new earth symbolizes the absence of tumultuous conflict.

C. "And I saw the holy city, new Jerusalem, coming down out of heaven from God, prepared as a bride adorned for her husband. And I heard a loud voice from the throne saying, 'Behold, the dwelling place of God is with man. He will dwell with them, and they will be his people, and God himself will be with them as their God. He will wipe away every tear from their eyes, and death shall be no more, neither shall there be mourning nor crying nor pain anymore, for the former things have passed away'" (Rev. 21:2–4).
   1. These are the blessings for which the people of God can look forward to with joyful expectation.

   2. The threat of death hangs over the head of every human.

3. One day the last enemy, death, will be destroyed.

D. The Christian can rejoice in the knowledge that through Christ's victory over the grave death is defeated.
    •   Jesus rose from the grave as a demonstration of God's same promise of resurrection to the believer.

E. The image of God wiping away our tears permanently is one of Scripture's most powerful descriptions of God comforting us and forever removing our sorrows.
    1. God will remove our pain and discomfort and then make all things new.

    2. God will not destroy the old, but rather redeem, renew, perfect, and glorify the old.

    3. God will not destroy the earth, but rather restore it to perfection.

F. John is commanded to write down the visions he sees because the trustworthy words of God need to be preserved for future generations.

G. "And he who was seated on the throne said, 'Behold, I am making all things new.' Also he said, 'Write this down, for these words are trustworthy and true.' And he said to me, 'It is done! I am the Alpha and the Omega, the beginning and the end. To the thirsty I will give from the spring of the water of life without payment . . .' Then came one of the seven angels who had the seven bowls full of the seven last plagues and spoke to me, saying, 'Come, I will show you the Bride, the wife of the Lamb.' And he carried me away in the Spirit to a great, high mountain, and showed me the holy city Jerusalem coming down out of heaven from God, having the glory of God" (Rev. 21:5–6; 9–11a).
    1. The old Jerusalem was a city of dust whereas the New Jerusalem will be a city adorned with the glory of God.

    2. John gives a detailed description of the glories of the New Jerusalem in chapter 21.

H. The prevalence of symbols in apocalyptic literature is to point to a reality greater than itself.
    •   John's description of the New Jerusalem is breathtaking yet still falls short of the reality he is trying to describe.

I. "And I saw no temple in the city, for its temple is the Lord God the Almighty and the Lamb" (Rev. 21:22).
    1. The temple represented the presence of God amidst His people in Jewish thought.

2. The temple is an outward manifestation of the reality of God Himself.

J. "And the city has no need of sun or moon to shine on it, for the glory of God gives it light, and its lamp is the Lamb" (Rev. 21:23).
   1. The sun is a source of light and warmth to the earth.

   2. The brightness, brilliance, and warmth of the Lamb is greater than the sun itself.

K. Man is overwhelmed in Scripture when the glory of God breaks into his life.
   1. Man was destined for glory when he was formed from the dust.

   2. Those who put their faith in Christ will one day partake of God's glory.

L. The life story of the redeemed is not dust to dust, but rather dust to glory.

BIBLE STUDY

1. How does Revelation 12 introduce the second half of the book? How is the conflict in the heavens translated into a conflict on the earth?

2. Contrast the sealing of the righteous in Revelation 7 with the marking of the unbelieving by the beast in chapter 13. What is the significance of these signs?

3. Why is the symbol of the wedding feast in Revelation 19:7 an appropriate image to celebrate Christ's victory with the saints over Satan? How does the great prostitute provide a striking contrast with the bride clothed in white?

4. Revelation 20:10 describes the future of the Devil, the Beast, and the False Prophet. How might the knowledge that the anti-Christian forces of the world (both political and religious) as well as their ringleader the Devil himself, will be destroyed bring comfort to those enduring severe persecution in the first century? Read Revelation 6:9–11. How is the scene in chapter 20 an answer to their prayers? How might this encourage the church in any age when it finds itself persecuted?

5. How is the Holy City described in 21:2? How might the preparations of a wedding help you grasp what John is saying using this imagery? Where will the Holy City be located?

6. Compare Genesis 17:7, Exodus 6:7, and Leviticus 26:11–12 to Revelation 21:3. The three Old Testament passages affirm the ultimate blessings of the covenant. How might this hope comfort you in times of despair and give you confidence for the future? How does Revelation 21:3, when compared to the Old Testament passages, show God's faithfulness?

DISCUSSION

1. Notice how Revelation 21:6–7 links taking freely the water of life and overcoming. How does this contrast to the list in 21:8? What does this indicate about the nature of true believers in Christ? Look over the list in 21:8 and consider the culture you encounter every day. What will be missing from it if this passage is fulfilled?

2. Read Revelation 21:9–24 and think of the most exquisite jewelry you have ever seen. According to 21:27, who will inherit this city? How would this challenge the original audience to examine their own faith? What is the connection between God's choosing and our obedience?

3. What is the exhortation of the Spirit of God and the church, Christ's bride, in 22:17? What are you doing to "Come!" to the spiritual feasts of God for you? What do you do to flee from them? How can you use the material in the concluding chapters of Revelation to challenge those around you to come to the One who gives the water of life freely?

FOR FURTHER STUDY

Bauckham, Richard. *The Theology of the Book of Revelation*
Beale, G.K. *The Book of Revelation*
Johnson, Dennis E. *Triumph of the Lamb*
Mathison, Keith A. *From Age to Age*